I0759968

LIT UP INSIDE / KEEP 'ER LIT

Lit Up Inside / Keep 'Er Lit
The Collected Lyrics

VAN MORRISON

edited by EAMONN HUGHES
foreword by JOHN COOPER CLARKE

faber

First published in the UK in 2025
by Faber & Faber Limited
The Bindery, 51 Hatton Garden
London EC1N 8HN
Published in the USA in 2025

Typeset by Faber & Faber Ltd
Printed in the UK by CPI Group (UK) Ltd, Croydon CR0 4YY

A CIP record for this book
is available from the British Library

ISBN 978-0-571-39801-0

Printed and bound in the UK on FSC® certified paper in line with our continuing commitment to ethical business practices, sustainability and the environment.
For further information see faber.co.uk/environmental-policy

Our authorised representative in the EU for product safety is
Easy Access System Europe, Mustamäe tee 50, 10621 Tallinn, Estonia
gpsr.requests@easproject.com

10 9 8 7 6 5 4 3 2 1

Contents

Foreword *by John Cooper Clarke* xiii

LIT UP INSIDE

Introduction *by Eamonn Hughes* 3

The Story of Them 13
Gloria 16
My Lonely Sad Eyes 18
Mystic Eyes 19
Philosophy 20
Brown Eyed Girl 21
T.B. Sheets 23
Spanish Rose 25
Who Drove the Red Sports Car? 27
Send Your Mind 28
The Back Room 30
Joe Harper Saturday Morning 33
Madame George 35
Slim Slow Slider 38
The Way Young Lovers Do 39
Moondance 41
Into the Mystic 43
Brand New Day 44
Crazy Face 46
I've Been Workin' 47
Blue Money 49
Street Choir 51
Tupelo Honey 53
When that Evening Sun Goes Down 55
Jackie Wilson Said (I'm in Heaven When You Smile) 56

Gypsy 58
Listen to the Lion 60
Saint Dominic's Preview 62
Snow in San Anselmo 65
Warm Love 66
Hard Nose the Highway 68
Wild Children 70
The Great Deception 71
Bulbs 73
Comfort You 75
Come Here My Love 76
Cul-de-Sac 77
It Fills You Up 78
Cold Wind in August 80
Kingdom Hall 82
Wavelength 85
Bright Side of the Road 87
Rolling Hills 89
And the Healing Has Begun 91
You Know What They're Writing About 94
Summertime in England 97
Celtic Ray 104
Dweller on the Threshold (Van Morrison and Hugh Murphy) 106
Beautiful Vision 108
She Gives Me Religion 110
Cleaning Windows 112
Higher Than the World 114
River of Time 116
Cry for Home 117
Rave on, John Donne/Rave on, Part Two 119
Tore Down à la Rimbaud 123
Got to Go Back 125
In the Garden 127
One Irish Rover 129
Foreign Window 130

Tir Na Nog 132
I Forgot that Love Existed 134
Someone Like You 135
Alan Watts Blues 137
Did Ye Get Healed? 139
Irish Heartbeat 141
Whenever God Shines His Light 143
Have I Told You Lately that I Love You? 145
Coney Island 147
Orangefield 148
These Are the Days 150
So Quiet in Here 151
In the Days Before Rock 'n' Roll (Van Morrison and Paul Durcan) 153
Memories 155
Why Must I Always Explain? 157
See Me Through Part II (Just a Closer Walk with Thee) 158
Take Me Back 160
All Saints Day 163
Hymns to the Silence 164
On Hyndford Street 166
Too Long in Exile 168
Wasted Years (Duet with John Lee Hooker) 170
No Religion 172
Songwriter 174
Days Like This 175
Fire in the Belly 176
Burning Ground 178
Sometimes We Cry 180
Not Supposed to Break Down 181
Madame Joy 183
Naked in the Jungle 186
The Street Only Knew Your Name 187
Show Business 189
Philosopher's Stone 192
High Summer 194

Choppin' Wood 196
What Makes the Irish Heart Beat 198
What's Wrong with This Picture? 200
Somerset 202
Meaning of Loneliness 203
Stranded 205
Pay the Devil 206
This Has Got to Stop 207
End of the Land 209
Song of Home 210
Soul 212
Mystic of the East 213

KEEP 'ER LIT

Introduction *by Eamonn Hughes* 217

If You and I Could Be As Two 225
Bad or Good 227
Could You Would You 229
Friday's Child 230
One Two Brown Eyes 232
You Just Can't Win 233
The Smile You Smile 235
Astral Weeks 236
Sweet Thing 239
And It Stoned Me 241
Crazy Love 243
Caravan 244
Come Running 246
These Dreams of You 248
Everyone 250
Domino 251
Virgo Clowns 253
If I Ever Needed Someone 255

Wild Night 257
I Wanna Roo You (Scottish Derivative) 259
I Will Be There 261
Redwood Tree 262
Autumn Song 264
Mechanical Bliss 267
Fair Play 269
Linden Arden Stole the Highlights 271
Who Was That Masked Man? 272
Streets of Arklow 273
You Don't Pull No Punches but You Don't Push the River 275
Gotta Make It through the World 277
The Eternal Kansas City 279
Joyous Sound 281
Flamingos Fly 283
Checkin' It Out 285
Natalia 287
Lifetimes 289
Hungry for Your Love 291
Take It Where You Find It 293
Full Force Gale 297
You Make Me Feel So Free 299
Steppin' Out Queen 301
Troubadours 303
Satisfied 305
Wild Honey 307
When Heart Is Open 309
Haunts of Ancient Peace 311
Northern Muse (Solid Ground) 312
Inarticulate Speech of the Heart 313
A Sense of Wonder 314
Oh the Warm Feeling 316
A Town Called Paradise 317
Queen of the Slipstream 319
Give Me My Rapture 321
Contacting My Angel 322

I'd Love to Write Another Song 323
I'm Tired Joey Boy 324
Daring Night 325
Real Real Gone 328
Enlightenment 330
Youth of 1000 Summers 332
Professional Jealousy 334
I'm Not Feeling It Anymore 336
Some Peace of Mind 338
Village Idiot 339
Carrying a Torch 341
Pagan Streams 343
I Need Your Kind of Loving 344
Big Time Operators 346
Perfect Fit 348
Ancient Highway 350
In the Afternoon 353
Rough God Goes Riding 355
This Weight 357
Waiting Game 359
Piper at the Gates of Dawn 361
It Once Was My Life 363
The Healing Game 365
Wonderful Remark 367
Don't Worry about Tomorrow 369
Try for Sleep 370
Drumshanbo Hustle 372
Goin' Down Geneva 374
In the Midnight 375
When the Leaves Come Falling Down 376
Precious Time 378
Golden Autumn Day 380
Meet Me in the Indian Summer 382
Whatever Happened to PJ Proby? 384
The Beauty of the Days Gone By 386
Man Has to Struggle 388

Fast Train 390
Whinin' Boy Moan 392
Too Many Myths 394
Goldfish Bowl 396
Little Village 398
Once in a Blue Moon 400
Get on with the Show 401
Fame 403
Celtic New Year 405
Magic Time 407
Blue and Green 409
Behind the Ritual 411
How Can a Poor Boy? 414
Open the Door (to Your Heart) 416
Goin' Down to Monte Carlo 418
Born to Sing 419
Close Enough for Jazz 421
Retreat and View 422
Pagan Heart 424
In Tiburon 427
Look Beyond the Hill 429
Memory Lane 430
The Pen Is Mightier than the Sword 432
Transformation 434
Broken Record 435
5am Greenwich Mean Time 437
Ain't Gonna Moan No More 439
Love Is Hard Work 441
Spirit Will Provide 443
The Prophet Speaks 444

Acknowledgements 447
Index of Titles and First Lines 449

Foreword *by John Cooper Clarke*

I have been called upon to explain the inexplicable, i.e. to capture the ongoing allure of Mr George Ivan Morrison. Van the Man, spelled M–A–N. But how to encapsulate his unique finesse using only the blunt instrument of mere language? This requires the subjective approach.

My introduction to his work began the year I left school. It happened like this . . .

'The Weekend Starts Here' – has there ever been a more joyful slogan? This wake-up call preceded the opening credits for *Ready Steady Go!*, the governor teen TV spectacular of 1964, featuring dance steps, wardrobe advice and music, music, music. All the socially mobile superstars, plus many of the Stateside artists they championed: Solomon Burke, John Lee Hooker, Betty Everett, Wilson Pickett, Inez and Charlie Foxx, Screamin' Jay Hawkins and more. James Brown even! The signature tune was 'Baby, Please Don't Go' by Them. Star vocalist – Van Morrison. His off-camera impact, established by virtue of his souped-up version of this Chicago blues standard, ushered in the restless spirit of the next two days – the weekend starts here. The point is, I heard the man before any photographic evidence presented itself. A purely sonic connection, which, for me, is possible only with a singer.

I believe that excellence can only be perceived within a tradition and, the way my fifteen-year-old mind had it figured, Them were part of the moodier end of the emerging R&B scene, with a side order of mood. That demi-monde was exemplified by certain metropolitan nightclubs, like the Bag O'Nails, the Hundred Club, the Marquee and the Flamingo, home of Georgie Fame and the Blue Flames.

As a provincial trainee beatnik on a tight budget, these joints, and the crepuscular life they represented, were all the more glamorous for being at a considerable remove. Manchester had its equivalents, however, contenders of a variable standard. Some were overcrowded, under-ventilated, sub-street-level dungeons, putrid, pestiferous and grim. You couldn't fault the music policy, but you wouldn't find a woman in there. Higher up the food chain you had Club 43, the Blue Note and the Twisted Wheel, for example. Basements, yes, but made over nice and nice. The dress code was stylish. They were often unlicensed, so, refreshments-wise, it was goofballs and Coca-Cola or nothing.

It was at one such venue, the Oasis, that I first encountered Them and their one and only focal point, Van Morrison, in a dogtooth sports coat, dark blue parallel cords and high-heel Chelsea boots, his hair a wild cascade of copper-coloured curls. You get only one chance to make a first impression. Then there was the voice, the sonorous instrument of a man much older than his nineteen years.

They opened with 'Baby, Please Don't Go', as heard on TV, segueing into the B-side, 'Gloria', self-composed a year earlier and an immediate signifier of his prodigious talent, with its slow and slinky build-up, sliding into its feverish climax. No wonder it's a classic. All this, plus a preview of their next single.

'Here Comes the Night', written by Burt Berns, is an early example of the singer's emotional reach as, despite his urgent and emphatic style, he perfectly conveys his bitter distress over a wayward girlfriend. Those five romantic, twangy guitar notes recur throughout the song in order to announce the titular phrase, while the rest of the lyric deals with an inner dialogue of treachery, loneliness and a painful, obsessive dread of the fast-approaching twilight. Directly from his shattered heart to you. At that point my girlfriend Sheila and I had recently fallen apart, so I was borderline emotional.

From that day to this Van Morrison has been a regular on the soundtrack of my life. Who could ever get over *Astral Weeks*, for instance? Four years and a thousand miles from Them, an album like no other, with its shimmering orchestration, inspired arrangements and Van Morrison, expertly pitched in every department of this attractively mysterious exercise. Time and space forbid further analysis, and anyway, in the words of the late Bill Withers, 'The composition of a song requires a kind of magic that I don't care to mess with.' Amen.

Van Morrison has walked down many musical boulevards since Cyprus Avenue and richly deserves his international clout. With a bagful of hits, his career spans sixty-two years and continues, by popular demand, to go from strength to strength. You can't argue with that.

'All sport aspires to boxing,' said Ernest Hemingway. To paraphrase, I reckon all art aspires to poetry in its quest to haunt the hearts of strangers. As a professional poet, I would say that, wouldn't I? However, this bold aspiration is lavishly omnipresent, right here in the work of this most singular songsmith. Van Morrison's lyrics continue to hold the listener in their thrall, and here they are, encased within these covers. 445 pages of pure gold.

LIT UP INSIDE

Introduction *by Eamonn Hughes*

Any significant writer creates their own world. Van Morrison has certainly done this through his music, which, as the playwright Stewart Parker put it, is an 'amalgam of urban styles which Morrison has made his own'. This book exists because Morrison has also created a world through his words. It is a world of back streets and mystic avenues; memories of childhood wonder and of adult work suffuse it; it is a place where the chime of church bells and the playing of the radio break a silence that can be sometimes stifling, at other times spiritual. It is a world generously peopled (in all senses of that phrase), but solitude and the benefits of being 'cloud-hidden' are never overlooked. Here love exists but may not last in either its divine or earthly forms. It is a place of sharp dealing but also of consolation, comfort and even grace. It is a world bounded by the river and the railway line, though these are means of passage as much as boundaries. The river and the railway are key features of the lexicon of twentieth-century popular music but, in their opposition of the natural and the man-made, they also echo the famous definition by Louis MacNeice (himself influenced by various forms of popular music) of Belfast being located between the 'mountains and the gantries'. Belfast is, then, as good a name as any for the world that we find in Morrison's words, but, as with MacNeice's poetry and Parker's plays, though Belfast may begin as a real place, it is ultimately more important as a site of the imagination. As such, it is not confined to the actual city of that name but is instead a terrain that can expand and contract as creative needs dictate.

This volume is made up of about a third of Morrison's work over a fifty-year career, and it aims to be a representative selection of that work. It begins and ends with versions of Belfast: 'The Story of Them' and 'Mystic of the East'. These are rooted in the city in which Morrison was born and grew up, and to which he has returned. Those bare biographical facts tell us little, however, about how Belfast is made and remade throughout his writing. The Belfast that has appeared in so many headlines during Morrison's life has also generated more than its share of remarkable writers over the last fifty years, but Morrison can stand shoulder to shoulder with them as someone who has not merely described his city, but rather shaped and moulded it to his own artistic ends.

'The Story of Them', one of the earliest lyrics gathered here, demonstrates just how soon he was doing this and with what degree of originality. It provides a map of the city like no other before it (and few since). This is a lyric written from within the moment and presents a version of Belfast recorded nowhere else: it's a Belfast in which the move from the Spanish Rooms on the Falls to the Maritime Hotel, just off the city centre, acknowledges no sectarian division. Instead, in this version of Belfast it is long hair and perceived scruffiness which are the markers of difference: this is a city mapped by music. While this may seem unremarkable – popular music in all its forms has, after all, consistently used place names – in the post-war years when America began to export new and exciting forms of music it was hard, on the eastern seaboard of the Atlantic, not to associate the originality and excitement of that music with the places in which it was set. So the names roll through the music as it develops from Mississippi to Chicago, from Kansas City to Broadway, from Memphis to Detroit, from New Orleans to New York. What Morrison understood before almost anyone else was that such places were not remote for those writing about them; these were the streets, rivers, cities and landscapes outside their doors. This involved recognising the places of popular music not as the exoticised landscapes of a glamorously foreign America, but rather as the often ambivalently welcoming places within which lives are lived and find expression. Given this, the blues can then roll down

Royal Avenue just as readily as along the Mississippi and into Chicago. Morrison was therefore ahead of many of his contemporaries – Lennon and McCartney, Ray Davies, Jagger and Richards – in making lyrical use of his own place. (Chuck Berry, after all, wrote about Liverpool before the Beatles did.) To say that Morrison invented a Lagan Delta may seem improbable until one remembers that Belfast is a city of many rivers – the Beechie, the Connswater and the Lagan are all named in his songs – and these are matched by the variety of music that flows through its streets in his imagining of it. This intuition about place is all the more remarkable when one thinks of the history of poetry in Belfast and Northern Ireland. The story of that poetry often involves a search for predecessors who can, in the face of pressure from metropolitan centres, enable the use of a local territory for imaginative purposes; so Seamus Heaney looks back to Patrick Kavanagh, just as Paul Muldoon looks back to Heaney. Morrison, under the considerable cultural pressure of the emergence of a new, American-oriented popular culture and operating on his own terms, comes early to an understanding of the value of his own place, and is in turn then able to give expression to the experience of that place.

None of this is to say that Belfast is in any way a confined location. As with any deeply imagined terrain it has its specific features, yet can open out to encompass anything and everything that creativity may need to call on. It can be as small as a room or a backyard, or as open-ended as a threshold on to wonder. Even as he was asserting the right of the real Belfast as a fit location for his lyrics, Morrison was also beginning to see through and beyond it. Belfast is the first location for the visionary aspects of Morrison's writing as it moves from the everyday into the possibility of the extraordinary; from his earliest writing, back streets can turn into mystic avenues. The city is then made to yield to a form of what we have to call urban pastoral when transformed by everyday vision. In that phrase we also have to understand that the visionary is elevating and celebrating the everyday.

Belfast is also filtered through many song styles. The conventions governing the lyrics of the blues are different from those of the soul ballad and different again from the country-and-western song, to pick just three styles. In this volume these styles are to be seen in the different shapes that the lyrics make on the page, from the brevity and repetition of 'Mystic Eyes', through the rolling variations of 'Summertime in England' and the way in which the spoken section of 'See Me Through Part II' breaks into the regularity of the hymn form, to the formality on the page of 'Songwriter'. Each song style answers to different imperatives, satisfies different needs. In each instance, the writer has to balance the need to stay close enough to the convention to keep the style recognisable while also challenging and stretching those conventions. In Morrison's case the popular song, in whatever form, is constantly challenged and stretched: the aim, to adapt a phrase of Seamus Heaney's, is to make it eat stuff it has never eaten before. Partly because so many of the forms in which he works are, as he knows, deep-rooted, Morrison's voice has a maturity and an interest in matters which go beyond those usually thought of as the preserve of the song lyric.

In none of this, then, can we say that his writing is confined to a specific locale. In using Belfast (and, later, other Northern Irish places), Morrison's lyrics move in two directions: drilling down and back into origins and memories, and surging outwards in ever-expanding waves to other places and to that territory which is beyond place. On the one hand, the details of his city are associated with the many musics first heard there. These were both local (Orange bands, Salvation Army bands, gospel and praise music, hymns and folk music) and what we now think of as American (jazz, blues, rhythm and blues, gospel and soul). But the traffic between America and Belfast is long-standing. Emigrants from Ireland, many carrying their music with them, have been settling in America for centuries, and Belfast was one of the first places where the newly formed, post-revolutionary United States established a trade consulate. In the post-war period, as one of the war children, this connection was most obviously experienced by Morrison through records (and his father's collection has achieved almost legendary status), and even more particularly through the radio, which is, in its different guises – 'wireless', 'wavelength' and 'ether' are some of its other names in the songs – one of the recurrent features of Morrison's writing. It is always an immediate, even comforting presence: in that remarkable song 'T.B. Sheets', radio becomes the only possible consolation – 'I turned on the radio / If you wanna hear a few tunes, I'll turn on the radio for you / There you go, there you go, there you go, baby, there you go'. The radio in Morrison's writing is not the voice of some remote central authority, but rather an intimate presence bringing music from many different places (American music via European stations), and many of the features of that music, far from being in opposition to the 'Sunday-school culture' associated with local forms of music, have their roots in that culture. Radio and its correlates represent forms of connection, of both reception and transmission. The world outside comes sweeping in and is then sent rippling back out in a movement of contraction and expansion.

Morrison's recognition that the music which came to him through records and the radio has a kinship with and owes debts to the music of the streets, churches and tin tabernacles of his childhood enables him to distil the city into its abstract components – such as the train and the river (to take the title of Jimmy Giuffre's theme music from *Jazz on a Summer's Day*) – and use these to build a more expansive landscape. Belfast, too, can be taken and rendered into symbolic, even mythologised places. In this way Belfast is a constantly expanding territory: its borders are tested, its limits are stretched. So when the scene of the songs moves, as it does, to other places – London, Buffalo, Boston, San Francisco, England in summertime – it's not that they have nothing new to offer so much as that they are encountered as already familiar, known in advance and accepted for what they might add to the imaginative terrain. By the time of 'Saint Dominic's Preview', for example, 'the chains, badges, flags and emblems' of Belfast are seen to be on an equal footing with the archetypal blues location of the crossroads and the crying railroad trains of country music: 'And for every cross-country corner / For every Hank Williams railroad train that cries / And all the chains, badges, flags and emblems . . .'

Belfast, in Morrison's imaginative encounters with it, has an expansive quality, then, and while by no means all of his lyrics are to be thought of as literally located in the city and its environs – the room in 'Gloria' or the 'old graveyard' of 'Mystic Eyes' could be anywhere – it remains the foundational location, the place where music first played and thus enabled the expansion into all other places. So when Morrison's lyrics move outwards and away from Belfast, 'way up to Caledonia', say, that movement is both outwards towards a mythical pan-Scottish territory and yet carries with it the memory of Louis Jordan's 'Caldonia' (which Morrison has covered). The lyrics journey towards more recognisably American landscapes, but there is no sense of being either overawed or of simply offering the scale and unfamiliarity of these places as interesting in their own right. Instead there is a near-paradoxical sense of familiarity rooted in pre-existing knowledge derived from music and literature absorbed initially in Belfast: 'I heard Leadbelly and Blind Lemon / On the street where I was born / Sonny Terry, Brownie McGhee and/Muddy Waters . . . / I went home and read . . . / Kerouac's *Dharma Bums* and *On the Road*'. The songs of America, as we might call them, can, then, stand beside the deep American pastoral of *Basement Tapes*-era Bob Dylan and the first albums of The Band. Like them, though he has come from much further away, Morrison understands the deep roots of these songs and knows that the sweetness of Tupelo honey is given some of its savour by the bitterness of Tupelo blues.

The other element that enters the lyrics at this time, despite the temptations of American pastoral, is a hard-edged rejection of the too-easy comforts of a counter-culture peopled by those ultimately 'determined / Not to feel anyone else's pain'. The blandishments and deceptions of the music business are a frequent and justified target of Morrison's songs, distractions from the real work of being a 'Songwriter', which, as with cleaning windows in his youth, is a matter of being 'a working man in my prime'. Against the music business's sharp practices, we have to consider the generosity of Morrison's lyrics: they are richly populated by a cast of formative influences, cultural icons and contemporaries. Any reader of these words can acquire an extraordinary musical education simply by noting the names of other musicians and singers. What most of these names have in common is the fact that, confronted with a sharp-edged and often punitive world, they too sought for ways to express both the details of that world and to reach for something beyond it. Whether these figures are defined as blues or soul or rock-and-roll singers, their origins are most often in forms of sacred music. Consequently, in their music there is a frequently unresolved tension between celebrating such joys as are to be found in a hard, secular world and a striving to express something beyond that world. Looking at the many literary names that pepper such songs as 'Rave on, John Donne' in this context makes one realise that these writers are named too because they share this irresolution between the sanctified and the sinful.

No matter how specific his songs are, how rooted in this world, there is always that element of searching for that which lies beyond. It's there from the start in 'Mystic Eyes' (and could the name 'Gloria' really have been chosen at random? Like the greatest of soul songs there is an aching ambiguity in many of Morrison's lyrics as they slide back and forth between the sacred and secular) and it continues throughout his writing. There are songs here which reach, however uncertainly, for something which cannot be articulated. Another feature of the writing is just how often it courts silence. 'On Hyndford Street' (a phrase from which provides the title for these selected lyrics) is notable for its concern not only with the sounds but also the silences of Belfast. If Morrison's music is a compound of the urban sounds itemised here – the wireless playing Radio Luxembourg, the railway, 'Sunday six bells', 'Debussy', 'voices echoing late at night over Beechie River' – then the words are trying to capture, here and elsewhere, a kind of living silence. Anyone who has seen Morrison perform live will know that he plays with the full dynamic range available to him: he and his band can switch from full-throated roar to stealth mode, as if trying to play silence itself. His words, too, attempt this impossibility – silence runs through them. It's there in the last lyric collected here, 'Mystic of the East': 'I can't find any reason to speak'. But this song also returns us to the streets of 'Cleaning Windows', in which he is earning a living and, away from manual labour, developing interests in mysticism and music and literature. If Belfast is known for political violence and, prior to that, for being an industrial city, Morrison's words offer an alternative to the first and an all too rare glimpse of the second: accounts of physical labour are still remarkably rare in all kinds of writing. But what they also suggest is that even somewhere as apparently unpromising as industrial east Belfast, Morrison's original stamping ground, can be offered as a place of potential spiritual wonder. Taken as a whole, Morrison's words, then, offer those things that we look for in popular song, but they also offer so much more.

It is for others to interpret the details of these songs as they see fit, for others to argue the merits of those interpretations. Despite the temptations of such argument, what I've tried to offer here is a map of the world of Van Morrison's lyrics. Some will find it useful, I hope, as a guide to some of the features of that world. Others may well find it more pleasurable and instructive simply to get lost in this rich, expansive, many-peopled place, with its grittiness, its visions, its longing and loss, and its sense of deep fulfilment. Whichever way you choose to proceed, we can all, in this volume, follow the words as they 'rave on . . . on printed page'.

The Story of Them

When friends were friends
And company was right
We'd drink and talk and sing
All through the night
Morning came leisurely and bright
Downtown we'd walk
And passers-by
Would shudder with delight
Mmmmmm
Good times

At Izzie's, man
All the cats were there
Just dirty enough to say
'We don't care'
But the management had had complaints
About some cats with long, long hair
'Look, look, look'
And the people'd stare
'Why, you won't be allowed in anywhere'
Barred from pubs, clubs and dancing halls
Made the scene at the Spanish Rooms on the Falls
And, man, four pints of that stuff was enough to have you
Out of your mind
Climbing, climbing up the walls
Out of your mind
But it was a gas, all the same
Mmmmmm
Good times

Now just right about this time with the help of the three Js

Started playin' in the Maritime
That's Jerry, Jerry and Jimmy
And you know they were always fine
And they helped us run the Maritime
And don't forget Kit
Boppin' people on the head and knockin' them out
You know he did his bit and all
Was something else then
Mmmmmm
Good times

Now people say, 'Who are,
Or what are,
Them?'

That little one sings and that big one plays the guitar with a
Thimble on his finger, runs it up and down the strings
The bass player don't shave much
I think they're all a little bit touched
But the people came
And that is how we made our name
Too much, it was
Mmmmmm
Yeah, good times

Wild, sweaty, crude, ugly
And mad
And sometimes just a little bit sad
Yeah, they sneered and all
But up there, we just havin' a ball
It was a gas, you know
Lord
Some good times

We are Them, take it or leave it

Do you know they took it?
And it kept coming
And we worked for the people
Sweet sweat
And the misty, misty atmosphere
Gimme another drink of beer, baby
Gotta get goin' here
Because it was a gas
Lord
Good times

Blues come rollin'
Down Royal Avenue
Won't stop at the City Hall
Just a few steps away
You can look up at
Maritime Hotel
Just a little bit sad
Gotta walk away
Wish it well

Gloria

Like to tell you 'bout my baby
You know she comes around
Just about five feet four
From her head to the ground
You know she comes around here
Just about midnight
She make me feel so good, Lord
She make me feel alright

And her name is G–L–O–R–I–I–I–I
G–L–O–R–I–A – Gloria
G–L–O–R–I–A – Gloria
I'm gonna shout it all night
Gloria
I'm gonna shout it every day
Gloria

She comes around here
Just about midnight
She make me feel so good, Lord
She make me feel alright
Comes walkin' down my street
Comes up to my house
She knocks upon my door
And then she comes to my room
She make me feel alright
G–L–O–R–I–A
G–L–O–R–I–A

I'm gonna shout it all night
I'm gonna shout it every day

Yeah, yeah, yeah, yeah, yeah
It's so good
Alright
Just so good
Alright

My Lonely Sad Eyes

Fill me my cup
And I'll drink your sparkling wine
Pretend that everything is fine
Till I see your sad eyes
Throw me a kiss
Across a crowded room
Some sunny windswept afternoon
Is none too soon for me to miss my sad eyes
Not bad eyes or glad eyes
But you, my sad eyes

Fortunate and free
And there go you and I
Between the earth and sky
But who are you and I wonder why we do so?
My sad eyes
Lonely

Oh what a story
The moon in all its glory, the song I sing and everything
For you, my sad eyes

You'd better
Fill me my cup
And I'll drink your sparkling wine
Pretend that everything is fine
Till I see your sad eyes
Not bad eyes or glad eyes
But you, my sad eyes
My lonely sad eyes

Mystic Eyes

One Sunday mornin'
We went walkin'
Down by the old graveyard
In the mornin' fog
And looked into
Yeah

Those mystic eyes, mystic eyes, mystic eyes, mystic eyes
Mystic eyes, mystic eyes, mystic eyes, mystic eyes

Philosophy

Told you, darling, all along
I was right and you were wrong
Pleasin' you is so hard to do
Tried all night long to be true

Can't sow wild oats 'spect to gather corn
Can't take right and make it wrong
Told you, darlin', long time ago
You gotta reap what you sow
And what you sow, yeah
Gonna make you weep someday, someday, someday
Yeah, what you sow
Gonna make you weep

Tried to keep you satisfied
Broke my heart, hurt my pride
It's all over now s'far as I can see
It's a lonely road and a memory
Of daily walkin' and talkin' about you and me, can't you see
I said, daily walkin' and talkin'

Can't sow wild oats 'spect to gather corn
Can't take right and make it wrong
Told you, darlin', long time ago
You gotta reap what you sow
And what you sow, yeah
Gonna make you weep someday, someday, someday
Yeah, what you sow, yeah
Gonna make you weep
Someday

Brown Eyed Girl

Hey, where did we go, days when the rains came
Down in the hollow, playing a new game
Laughing and a-running, hey, hey
Skipping and a-jumping
In the misty morning fog with our, our hearts a-thumping
And you, my brown eyed girl
You, my brown eyed girl

Whatever happened, to Tuesday and so slow
Going down the old mine with the transistor radio
Standing in the sunlight laughing
Hiding behind a rainbow's wall
Slipping and a-sliding all along the waterfall
With you, my brown eyed girl
You, my brown eyed girl

Do you remember when we used to sing
Sha la la la la la la la la lala dee dah
Just like that
Sha la la la la la la la la lala dee dah
La dee dah

So hard to find my way, now that I'm all on my own
I saw you just the other day, my, how you have grown
Cast my memory back there, Lord
Sometimes I'm overcome thinking about
Making love in the green grass, behind The Stadium
With you, my brown eyed girl
You, my brown eyed girl

Do you remember when we used to sing

Sha la la la la la la la la lala dee dah
Laying in the green grass
Sha la la la la la la la la lala dee dah
Dee dah dee dah dee dah dee dah dee dah dee
Sha la la la la la la la la la la la
Dee dah la dee dah la dee dah la

T.B. Sheets

Now listen, Julie baby
It ain't natural for you to cry in the midnight
It ain't natural for you to cry way into midnight through
Until the wee small hours long 'fore the break of dawn
Oh Lord

Now, Julie, an' there ain't nothin' on my mind
More further 'way than what you're lookin' for
I see the way you jumped at me, Lord, from behind the door
And looked into my eyes
Your little star-struck innuendos
Inadequacies and foreign bodies
And the sunlight shining through the crack in the windowpane
Numbs my brain
And the sunlight shining through the crack in the windowpane
Numbs my brain, oh Lord

Ha, so open up the window and let me breathe
I said open up the window and let me breathe

I'm looking down to the street below, Lord, I cried for you
I cried, I cried for you

Oh Lord

The cool room, Lord, is a fool's room
The cool room, Lord, is a fool's room
And I can almost smell your T.B. sheets
And I can almost smell your T.B. sheets
On your sick bed

I gotta go, I gotta go
And she said, 'Please stay, I wanna, I wanna,
I want a drink of water, I want a drink of water,
Go in the kitchen get me a drink of water'
I said, 'I gotta go, I gotta go, baby'
I said, 'I'll send, I'll send somebody around later,
You know we got Janet comin' around here later
With a bottle of wine for you, baby, but I gotta go'

The cool room, Lord, is a fool's room
The cool room, Lord, Lord, is a fool's room, a fool's room
And I can almost smell your T.B. sheets
I can almost smell your T.B. sheets, T.B.

I gotta go, I gotta go
I'll send around, send around one that grumbles later on,
  baby
We'll see what I can pick up for you, you know
Yeah, I got a few things going on too
Don't worry about it, don't worry about it, don't worry
Huh uh, go, go, go, I've gotta go, gotta go, gotta go, gotta go
Gotta go, gotta go, huh uh, alright, alright

I turned on the radio
If you wanna hear a few tunes, I'll turn on the radio for you
There you go, there you go, there you go, baby, there you go

You'll be alright too
I know it ain't funny, it ain't funny at all, baby
Always laying in the cool room, man, laying in the cool room
In the cool room, in the cool room

Spanish Rose

The wine beneath the bed
The things we've done and said
And all the memories that come glancing back to me
In my loneliness
Standing in the breach
The arms outstretched, but out of reach
And consciousness has found me sometimes wondering
Where you're at
Take me back again
Take me back one more time, Spanish rose

The way you pulled the gate
Behind you when you said, 'It ain't too late
Come on, let's swing the town and have a
Ball tonight'
And hoping you'd come through
And many others too
And all the friends we used to have in days gone by
I'm wondering
If you'll take me back again
Take me back one more time, Spanish rose

And when the lights went out
And no one was about, another country in full bloom
In the room we danced
And many hearts were torn
And when the word went around that everything was wrong
And just couldn't be put right
It tore me up, it tore me up, Lord

The way you held the note

The trembling in your throat
That just beginning of your wondrous smile
The rising of the water
The window into days gone by
I often ask myself and wonder why it's gone
Take me back again
Take me back one more time, Spanish rose

In slumber you did sleep
The window I did creep
And touch your raven hair and sang that song
Again to you
You did not even wince
You thought I was the prince
To come and take you from your misery
In lonely castle walls
Ah take me back again
Take me back one more time, Spanish rose

Who Drove the Red Sports Car?

Who drove the red sports car from the mansion
And laid upon the grass in summer time?
And who done me out high-time fashion
And made me read between the lines?
And who said, 'Follow the mile, you're only a child,
Sit on your throne, you got to make it on your own,
On your own'?

And who said, 'Ha, ha, look at you, look at you,
You got jam on your face'?
And who did your homework and read your Bible
And signed your name every place?
And who said, 'Fortunes untold don't go by gold,
You're much better known, you got to make it on your own,
On your own'?

And do you remember, do you remember this time?
I said a long time ago, when I came walkin' down
I came walkin' down, by Maggie's place
It started comin' on rain, it started comin' on rain
'Cause I had nothing on but a shirt and a pair of pants
And I was getting wet, I was getting wet, saturated, saturated
And Maggie opened up the window, and Jane swung out her
 right arm
She said, 'Hi!' I said, 'Hi, how're you doing, baby?'
She said, 'Come on in out the rain, come on in out the rain,
Lord, come on in out the rain, sit down by the fireside
And dry yourself.'
Achoo! Do it, do it, ha ha ha, I got caught
I got caught in a, in a bag, in the bag, oh Lord
I said, 'I don't mind if I do, I don't mind if I do'

Send Your Mind

Send your mind, send your mind
Send your mind, send your mind

While you're out there on the highway
Where the drivers roll on by
Going south between the bridges
Where the river's runnin' dry
And if you can't come home
Please send your mind

Send your mind, send your mind
Send your mind, send your mind

There you're talking, where you're going
On the train that ceased to roll
Across the nation, passing station
Where the night is black as coal
And if you can't come home
Please send your mind

Send your mind, send your mind
Send your mind, send your mind

With your hand laid on your heartbeat
And your head between the sheets
And the silence from the lamp post
On the corner of the street
And if you can't come home
Please send your mind

Send your mind, send your mind

Send your mind, send your mind
Send your mind, send your mind
Send your mind, send your mind

Ah little darlin', come on home
Come on home, ah send it, send it
Ah darlin', send it, baby
All you gotta do
Ah send it

The Back Room

In the back room, in the back room
I waited for you, you waited for me
The rain came down, pitter pat
Said, 'What, you think it's raining outside?'
Said, 'So what, turn the record player on'
Had a smoke, stood up, walked across to the john
In a cloud of mist, couldn't resist
Katie stepped in the hall, she grabbed the door
Found the key in the letterbox, she turned the door
Walked into the room, said, 'What's going on?

'I just got back from down the road,
I got a couple of bottles of wine, something to turn you on,
What'd you think about that?'
I said, 'Sit down, child,
Pull up a seat, you're soaking wet,
Take off your coat and hat, wipe your feet on the mat'
In the back room, in the back room
I waited for you, you waited for me

I said, 'What time it is, Johnny, where did we go all day?
Seem to get nowhere and do nothing
But sit looking at each other'
He said, 'I know, I've been doing the same thing for weeks'
I look at the clock and all of a sudden
I'm hypnotised and it speaks to me
And it goes tick-tock, tick-tock, tick-tock

And Katie said, 'I don't know what you gotta do
But I been working so hard lately
That I get home and just fall asleep in bed'

So we played some more sounds and grooved a while
Somebody brought out some cherry wine, cherry wine
And we talked about what was going on in the music world
And other things
Rain outside came down like it came never before
Down it came, down it came, rain, rain, rain
And I said, 'Baby, what time is it, what time is it,
Tell me, what time is it?'

'Four thirty'

So I peep round the corner of the blinds, and there you go
There's the little girls coming home from school
Looking so cool
Just learned their As to Zs
I said, 'Hey, man, don't that look funny, all of those girls
Coming home from school
And us sitting, talking and drinking
And all them other funny things?' Ha, ha

And Johnny said to me, 'You know what?'
I said, 'What?'
He said, 'Man, you gotta go out there and do something for yourself
You gotta go out and make
Or else you're gonna be sitting around here like nothing'
I said, 'You're right.' I said, 'You're so right'
He said, 'I know'
I said, 'Do ya?'
He said, 'You know you're cutting records, cutting records, right?
You can't do that and get through all the time.
You're gonna be out on the road
In the back seat, man, on the highway,
And the colours are gonna run.

All of a sudden don't you feel sick and the next day
You gotta make it?'
I said, 'Yeah, I feel sick'
I said, 'You know I can't stay here all the time,
As much as I'd like to
Just loon about all day and all night'
I decided to go down to the river
And watched the artist go through the motions

Gotta do my thing, gotta do my thing
In the back room, in the back room

Joe Harper Saturday Morning

When you thought I was a stranger
When you looked upon me
When I came back
But to take you from disaster
I cannot master the four winds in your shack
And the roamin' in the gloamin'
You have brought and set before me
And I think that it's an omen
I'm just not what so many people see

And you shined your glory all around
Did not disguise what you did
I asked you for half a pound, and you said
'Go see Joe Harper, Saturday morning, kid,
Go see Joe Harper, Saturday morning, kid'

And the child held the ball in the garden
With the old queen
And you kissed the lips that harden of a stranger
You know what I mean
And you walk down the streets so lonely
In your own childish way
And you thought that you would only
Do it for today

And you shined your glory all around
Did not disguise what we did
I asked you for half a pound, and you said
'Go see Joe Harper, Saturday morning, kid,
Go see Joe Harper, Saturday morning, kid'

And just outside the club
And the rain came down on his head
And he got all soaking wet
I said, 'Go for yourself,' and he said, 'I know, sure, sure,
I ain't conquered yet'
And I walked away from the backstreets in the rain and I saw
How many times that I die
And we turned on outside in the bus shelter
And I jumped on and said goodbye

And I shined my glory all around
Did not disguise what I did
Tried to keep it underground, but they said
'Go see Joe Harper, Saturday morning, kid,
Go see Joe Harper, Saturday morning, kid'

Madame George

Down on Cyprus Avenue
With the childlike visions leaping into view
Clicking clacking of the high-heeled shoe
Ford and Fitzroy and Madame George

Marching with the soldier boy behind
He's much older now, with hat on drinking wine
And that smell of sweet perfume comes drifting through
Early cool night air like Shalimar
And outside they're making all the stops
The kids out in the street collecting bottle tops
Gone for cigarettes and matches in the shops
Happy taking Madame George
Oh that's when you fall
Oh that's when you fall
Yeah, that's when you fall

When you fall into a trance
Sitting on a sofa playing games of chance
With your folded arms and history books you glance
Into the eyes of Madame George

And you think you've found the bag
You're getting weaker and your knees begin to sag
In a corner playing dominoes in drag
The one and only Madame George

And up from outside the frosty window raps
She jumps up and says, 'Lord have mercy,
I think that it's the cops'
And immediately drops everything she gots
Down into the street below

And you know you gotta go
On a train from Dublin up to Sandy Row
Throwing pennies at bridges down below
In the rain, hail, sleet and snow
Say goodbye to Madame George
Dry your eye for Madame George
Wonder why for Madame George

And as you leave, the room is filled with music
Laughing music, dancing music, all around the room
And all the little boys come round
Walking away from it all
So cool

And as you're about to leave
He jumps up 'n says, 'Hey, love,
You forgot your glove'
And the love that loves to love
That loves the love that loves
The love that loves to love
The love that loves to love
The love that loves

Say goodbye to Madame George
Dry your eyes for Madame George
Wonder why for Madame George
Dry your eyes for Madame George
Say goodbye

In the wind and the rain in the backstreet
In the backstreet
In the backstreet
Say goodbye to Madame George
In the backstreet
In the backstreet

In the backstreet
Well, down home
Down home in the backstreet
Gotta go
Say goodbye, goodbye, goodbye

Dry your eye, your eye, your eye
Your eye, your eye, your eye
Say goodbye to Madame George
And the love that loves to love
The love that loves to love

Say goodbye, goodbye, goodbye, goodbye
Say goodbye, goodbye, goodbye, goodbye
To Madame George
Dry your eyes for Madame George
Wonder why for Madame George
And the love that loves to love
The love that loves to love
Say goodbye, goodbye
Get on the train, darling
Get on the train, the train, the train, the train, the train,
darling
This is the train, this is the train, darling
This is the train
Oh say goodbye, goodbye, goodbye
Get on the train
Get on the train

Slim Slow Slider

Slim slow slider
Horse you ride is white as snow
Slim slow slider
Horse you ride is white as snow
Tell it everywhere you go

Saw you walking
Down by Ladbroke Grove this morning
Saw you walking
Down by Ladbroke Grove this morning
Catching pebbles for some sandy beach
You're out of reach

Saw you early this morning
With your brand-new boy and your Cadillac
Saw you early this morning
With your brand-new boy and your Cadillac
You're going for something and I know you
Won't be back

I know you're dying, baby
And I know you know it too
I know you're dying
And I know you know it too
Every time I see you
I just don't know what to do

The Way Young Lovers Do

We strolled through fields all wet with rain
And back along the lane again
Staring at the sunshine, in the sweet summertime
The way that young lovers do

I kissed you on the lips once more
And we said goodbye at your front door
In the night-time
That's the right time
To feel the way that young lovers do

Then we sat on our own star
And dreamed of the way that we were
And the way that we wanted to be
Then we sat on our own star
And dreamed of the way that I was for you
And you were for me

And then we danced the night away
And turning to each other say
'I love you,
I love you'
The way that young lovers do

Then we sat on our own star
And dreamed of the way that we were
And the way that we wanted to be
Then we sat on our own star
And dreamed of the way that I was for you
And you were for me

And we learned to dance the night away
Turning to each other say
'I love you,
Baby, I love you'
The way that young lovers do
Lovers do
Lovers do

Moondance

Well, it's a marvellous night for a moondance
With the stars up above in your eyes
A fantabulous night to make romance
'Neath the cover of October skies
And all the leaves on the trees are falling
To the sound of the breezes that blow
And I'm trying to please to the calling
Of your heart strings that play soft and low
And all the night's magic seems to whisper and hush
And all the soft moonlight seems to shine in your blush

Can I just have one more moondance with you, my love?
Can I just make some more romance with you, my love?

Well, I wanna make love to you tonight
I can't wait till the morning has come
And I know now the time is just right
And straight into my arms you will run
And when you come my heart will be waiting
To make sure that you're never alone
There and then all my dreams will come true, dear
There and then I will make you my own
And every time I touch you, you just tremble inside
And I know how much you want me that you can't hide

Can I just have one more moondance with you, my love?
Can I just make some more romance with you, my love?

Well, it's a marvellous night for a moondance
With the stars up above in your eyes
A fantabulous night to make romance

'Neath the cover of October skies
And all the leaves on the trees are falling
To the sound of the breezes that blow
And I'm trying to please to the calling
Of your heart strings that play soft and low
And all the night's magic seems to whisper and hush
And all the soft moonlight seems to shine in your blush

Can I just have one more moondance with you, my love?
Can I just make some more romance with you, my love?

One more moondance with you, in the moonlight
On a magic night
In the moonlight
On a magic night
Can I just have one more moondance with you, my love?

Into the Mystic

We were born before the wind
Also younger than the sun
And the bonnie boat was one as we sailed into the mystic
Hark, now hear the sailors cry
Smell the sea and feel the sky
Let your soul and spirit fly into the mystic

And when that foghorn blows I will be coming home
And when the foghorn blows I want to hear it
I don't have to fear it
And I want to rock your gypsy soul
Just like way back in the days of old
And magnificently we will fold into the mystic

When that foghorn blows you know I will be coming home
And when that foghorn whistle blows I gotta hear it
I don't have to fear it
And I want to rock your gypsy soul
Just like way back in the days of old
And together we will fold into the mystic

C'mon, girl
Too late to stop now

Brand New Day

When all the dark clouds roll away
And the sun begins to shine
I see my freedom from across the way
And it comes right in on time
Well, it shines so bright and it gives so much light
And it comes from the sky above
Make me feel so free, make me feel like me
And it lights my life with love

And it seems like, and it feels like
And it seems like, and it feels like
A brand new day
A brand new day

I was lost, double-crossed
With my hands behind my back
I was long-time hurt and thrown in the dirt
Shoved out on the railroad track
I've been used, abused and so confused
And I didn't have nowhere to run
But I stood and looked
And my eyes got hooked
On that beautiful morning sun

And it seems like, yes, it feels like
And it seems like, yes, it feels like
A brand new day
A brand new day

And the sun shines down all on the ground
Yeah, and the grass is oh so green

And my heart is still and I've got the will
And I don't really feel so mean
Here it comes, here it comes
Here it comes right now
And it comes right in on time
Well, it eases me and it pleases me
And it satisfies my mind

And it seems like, yes, it feels like
And it seems like, yes, it feels like
A brand new day
A brand new day

Crazy Face

All the people were waiting for Crazy Face
He said he'd meet them at his favourite place
Dressed in black satin, white linen and lace
With his head held high and a smile on his face

And he said
'Ladies and gentlemen, the prince is late'
As he stood outside the churchyard gate
And polished up on his .38 and said
'I got it from Jesse James'

All the people were waiting for Crazy Face
He said he'd meet them in his favourite place
Dressed in black satin, white linen and lace
With his head held high and a smile on his face

He said
'Ladies and gentlemen, the prince is late'
As he stood outside the churchyard gate
And polished up on his .38 and said
'I got it from Jesse James'

I've Been Workin'

I've been workin'
I've been workin' so hard
I've been workin'
I've been workin' so hard
I come home
Make love to you, make love to you

I've been grindin'
I've been grindin' so long
I've been grindin'
I've been grindin' so long

Been up the thruway
Down the thruway
Up the thruway, down the thruway
Up, down, back up again

I said woman, woman, woman, woman, woman, woman,
  woman, woman
Make me feel so good
Woman, woman, woman, woman, woman, woman, woman,
  woman
Make me feel alright
Alright, alright, alright, alright
Alright, alright, alright, alright
Alright, alright, alright, alright
Alright, alright, alright, alright

I said woman, woman, woman, woman, woman, woman,
  woman, woman
Make me feel so good

Woman, woman, woman, woman, woman, woman, woman,
woman
Make me feel alright
Alright, alright, alright, alright
Alright, alright, alright, alright
Alright, alright, alright, alright
Alright, alright, alright, alright

Make me feel so good
Set my soul on fire

Blue Money

The photographer smiles
Take a break for a while
Take a rest, do your very best
Take five, honey
Five, honey

Search in your bag
Light up a fag
Think it's a drag, but you're so glad
To be alive, honey
Live, honey

Say, when this is all over
You'll be in clover
We'll go out and spend
All of your blue money

Well, the cameraman smiles
Take a break for a while
Do your best, your very best
Take five, honey
Take five

Well, you search in your bag
Light up a fag
Think it's a drag, but you're so glad
To be alive, honey
Live, honey

Say, when this is all over
You'll be in clover

We'll go out and spend
All of your blue money

Say, when this is all over
We'll be in clover
We'll go out and spend
All your blue money

Blue money
Juice money
Loose money
Juice money
Loose money, honey
What kind of money, honey
Juice money
Loose money
Blue money

Street Choir

Street choir, sing me the song for the new day
Don't make it long and remember to sing it the old way
Let it all out, let your voice ring in the street now
My fun shall be this one to complete now

Why did you leave America?
Why did you let me down?
And now that things seem better off
Why do you come around?
You know I just can't see you now
In my New World crystal ball
You know I just can't free you now
That's not my job at all

Move it on up, move it on up by the window
Magnificent flow, let it all go in the moon glow
I'll take the wine, I'll take the wine with the gravy
Ask you the time and just send the bill to my baby

Why did you leave America?
Why did you let me down?
And now that things seem better off
Why do you come around?
You know I just can't see you now
In my new world crystal ball
You know I just can't free you now
That's not my job at all

Why did you leave America?
Why did you let me down?
And now that things seem better off

Why do you come around?
You know I just can't see you now
In my new world crystal ball
You know I just can't free you now
That's not my job at all
You know I just can't free you now
That's not my job at all

Tupelo Honey

You can take all the tea in China
Put it in a big brown bag for me
Sail right round all the seven oceans
Drop it straight into the deep blue sea

She's as sweet as Tupelo honey
She's an angel of the first degree
She's as sweet as Tupelo honey
Just like honey, baby, from the bee

You can't stop us on the road to freedom
You can't keep us 'cause our eyes can see
Men with insight, men in granite
Knights in armour bent on chivalry

She's as sweet as Tupelo honey
She's an angel of the first degree
She's as sweet as Tupelo honey
Just like honey, baby, from the bee

You can't stop us on the road to freedom
You can't stop us 'cause our eyes can see
Men with insight, men in granite
Knights in armour intent on chivalry

She's as sweet as Tupelo honey
She's an angel of the first degree
She's as sweet as Tupelo honey
Just like honey, baby, from the bee

She's alright, she's alright with me

You can take all the tea in China
Put it in a big brown bag for me
Sail it right round all the seven oceans
Drop it smack-dab in the middle of the deep blue sea

She's as sweet as Tupelo honey
She's an angel of the first degree
She's as sweet as Tupelo honey
Just like honey, baby, from the bee

Tell a tale of old Manhattan
Adirondack Trailways bus to go
And I'm waiting on my number
And I know my number's going to show

She's as sweet as Tupelo honey
She's an angel of the first degree
She's as sweet as Tupelo honey
Just like the real thing, from the bee

She's alright, she's alright with me

When that Evening Sun Goes Down

I want you to be around
When that evening sun goes down
I want you, be around
Keep my both feet on the ground
When that evening sun goes down
I want you, understand
Little girl, take me by my hand
I want you, understand
I wanna be your loving man
When that evening sun goes down

If it's nice, we'll go for a walk and a stroll in the clear moonlight
Singing a song, won't take long
Everything gonna be alright
And I wanna hold you oh so near
Keep you, darling, from all fear
I wanna hold you oh so near
Nibble on your little ear
When that evening sun goes down

If it's nice, go for a walk, stroll in the clear moonlight
Sing you a song, won't take long
Everything gonna be alright
And I wanna hold you oh so near
Keep you, darling, from all fear
I wanna hold you oh so near
Nibble on your little ear
When that evening sun goes down
When that evening sun goes down
When that evening sun goes down
When that evening sun goes down

Jackie Wilson Said (I'm in Heaven When You Smile)

Dadada da da da, dada da da da
Dadada da da da, dada da da da
Dadada da da da, dada da da da
Dadada da da da, dada da da da

Jackie Wilson said it was 'Reet Petite'
Kinda love you got, knock me off my feet
Let it all hang out, oh let it all hang out

And you know, I'm so wired up
Don't need no coffee in my cup
Let it all hang out, let it all hang out
Watch this

Ting-a-ling-a-ling, ting-a-ling-a-ling-ding
Ting-a-ling-a-ling, ting-a-ling-a-ling-ding
Do da do da do

I'm in heaven, I'm in heaven
I'm in heaven when you smile, when you smile
When you smile, when you smile

And when you walk across the room
You make my heart go, boom, boom, boom
Let it all hang out, baby, let it all hang out

And every time you look that way
Honey child, you make my day
Let it all hang out, what'd the man say, let it all hang out

Ting-a-ling-a-ling, ting-a-ling-a-ling-ding

Ting-a-ling-a-ling, ting-a-ling-a-ling-ding
Do da do da do

I'm in heaven, I'm in heaven
I'm in heaven when you smile, when you smile

I'm in heaven, I'm in heaven
I'm in heaven when you smile, one more time

I'm in heaven, I'm in heaven
I'm in heaven when you smile, when you smile

Gypsy

You can make out pretty good
When you're on your own
And you'll know just where you are
When you wanna roam

Got the moon above your head
And the road beneath your feet
Pull into a wooded glen
Make your own retreat

Li-a-di, di, di, di, di, di
Li-a-di, di, di, di, di, di
Li-a-di, di, di, di, di, di, di
Li-a-di, di, di, di, di, di
Li-a-di, di, di, di, di, di
Li-a-di, di, di, di, di, di, di
Gypsy

Laying underneath the stars
Can be so much fun
Especially when you're feeling good
When you're with the one you love

Sway to sounds of two guitars
Round the campfire bright
Then mellow out like violins
In the morning light

Li-a-di, di, di, di, di, di
Li-a-di, di, di, di, di, di
Li-a-di, di, di, di, di, di, di

Li-a-di, di, di, di, di, di
Li-a-di, di, di, di, di, di
Li-a-di, di, di, di, di, di, di
Gypsy

No matter where you wander
No matter where you roam
Any place you hang your hat
You know that that is home
Check it out first

Sway to sounds of two guitars
Round the campfire bright
Then mellow out like violins
In the morning light

Li-a-di, di, di, di, di, di
Li-a-di, di, di, di, di, di
Li-a-di, di, di, di, di, di, di
Li-a-di, di, di, di, di, di
Li-a-di, di, di, di, di, di
Li-a-di, di, di, di, di, di, di
Gypsy

Listen to the Lion

And all my love come down
All my love, come tumblin' down
All my love come tumblin' down
All my love, come tumblin' down

Oh listen to the lion
Oh listen, listen
To the lion
Sadly

And I shall search my soul
I shall search my very soul
And I shall search my very soul
I shall search my very soul

For the lion, for the lion
For the lion, for the lion
Inside of me

And all my tears have flown
All my tears, like water flow
And all my tears like water flow
All my tears, like water flow

For the lion, for the lion
For the lion, for the lion
Inside of me

Listen to the lion, listen to the lion
Listen to the lion, listen to the lion

And we sailed and we sailed
And we sailed and we sailed
And we sailed and we sailed
Sailed to Caledonia
And we sailed and we sailed
And we sailed and we sailed and we sailed
Way from Denmark, way up to Caledonia
Way from Denmark, way up to Caledonia
And we sailed and we sailed and we sailed
All around the world
And we sailed, and we sailed, and we sailed
Lookin' for a brand-new start
And we sailed, and we sailed, and we sailed
All around the world
Lookin' for a brand-new start, a brand-new start
Lookin' for a brand-new start, a brand-new start
And we sailed, and we sailed, and we sailed
And we sailed
Way from the Golden Gate
Way up to the New York City

Saint Dominic's Preview

Chamois cleaning all the windows
Singin' songs about Edith Piaf's soul
And I hear blue strains of 'Ne Regrette Rien'
Cross the street from Cathedral Notre Dame

Meanwhile back in San Francisco
I try hard to make this whole thing blend
And we sit upon this jagged
Story block with you my friend

And it's a long way to Buffalo
It's a long way to Belfast City too
And I'm hoping that Joyce won't blow the hoist
'Cause this time they bit off more than they can chew

As we gaze out on, as we gaze out on
As we gaze out on, as we gaze out on
Saint Dominic's Preview
Saint Dominic's Preview
Saint Dominic's Preview

All the orange boxes are scattered
Against the Safeway supermarket in the rain
And everybody feels so determined
Not to feel anyone else's pain

No one making no commitments
To anybody but themselves
Talkin' behind closed doorways
Trying to get outside empty shelves

And for every cross-country corner
For every Hank Williams railroad train that cries
And all the chains, badges, flags and emblems
And every strain on the brain and every eye

As we gaze out on, as we gaze out on
As we gaze out on, as we gaze out on
Saint Dominic's Preview
Saint Dominic's Preview
Saint Dominic's Preview

All the restaurant tables are completely covered
And the record company has paid out for the wine
You got everything in the world you ever wanted
And right about now your face should wear a smile

That's the way it all should happen
When you're in the state you're in
Have you got your pen and notebook ready
Think it's about time, time for us to begin

And meanwhile we're over in a 52nd Street apartment
Socialising with a wino few
I used to be hip and get wet with the jet set
But they was flyin' too high to see my point of view

As we gaze out on, as we gaze out on
As we gaze out on, as we gaze out on
Saint Dominic's Preview
Looked at the man
Saint Dominic's Preview
Looked at the band
Saint Dominic's Preview
Said their freedom marching out in the street
Freedom marching

Out in the street
Looked at the man
Turned around
Come back
Come back
Turned around
Looked at the man
Said, 'Hold on'
St Dominic's Preview
St Dominic's Preview
Soul meeting
St Dominic's Preview

Snow in San Anselmo

Snow in San Anselmo
And the deer cross by the lights
Of the mission down in old San Rafael
And a madman looking for a fight
A madman looking for a fight

And the massage parlour's open
And the clientele come and they go
And the classic-music station
Plays in the background soft and low
Plays in the background soft and low

And there's silence round the Cascades
And the air is crisp and clear
And the beginnings of the opera
Seem to suddenly appear
Seem to suddenly appear

And the pancake house is always crowded
Open twenty-four hours of every day
And if you suffer from insomnia
You can speed your time away
You can speed your time away

Snow in San Anselmo
My waitress, my waitress, my waitress
Said it was coming down
Said it hadn't happened in over thirty years
But it was laying on the ground
But it was laying on the ground

Warm Love

Look at the ivy on the old clinging wall
Look at the flowers and the green grass so tall
It's not a matter of when push comes to shove
It's just the hour on the wings of a dove
It's just warm love, it's just warm love

I dig it when you're fancy dressed up in lace
I dig it when you have a smile on your face
This inspiration's got to be on the flow
These invitations got to see it and know
It's just warm love, it's just warm love

And it's ever present everywhere, and it's ever present
  everywhere
That warm love
And it's ever present everywhere, and it's ever present
  everywhere
That warm love

To the country we're going
Lay and laugh in the sun
You can bring your guitar along
We'll sing some songs and have some fun

The sky is crying and it's time to go home
And we shall hurry to the car from the foam
Sit by the fire and dry out our wet clothes
It's raining outside from the skies up above
Inside it's warm love, inside it's warm love

And it's ever present everywhere, and it's ever present
everywhere
That warm love
And it's ever present everywhere, and it's ever present
everywhere
That warm love, can you feel it?

And it's ever present everywhere, and it's ever present
everywhere
That warm love
And it's ever present everywhere, and it's ever present
everywhere
That warm love

Hard Nose the Highway

Hey, kids, dig the first takes
Ain't that some interpretation
When Sinatra sings against Nelson Riddle strings
Then takes a vacation?

Seen some hard times, drawn some fine lines
No time for shoeshine, hard nose the highway

I was tore down at the Dead's place
Shaved head at the organ
But that wasn't half as bad as it was, oh no
Belfast and Boston

Seen some hard times, drawn some fine lines
No time for shoeshine, hard nose the highway

Put your money where your mouth is
Then we can get something going
In order to win you must be prepared to lose sometime
And leave one or two cards showing

Seen some hard times, drawn some fine lines
No time for shoeshine, hard nose the highway

Seen some hard times, drawn some fine lines
No time for shoeshine, hard nose the highway

Further on up the road
Further on up the road
It may not be today
It may be tomorrow

So if you live for today
Got to keep in mind
It may be tomorrow
Yes, further on up the road
Further on up
Further on up
Further on up
Further on up
Further on up
Further on
Up the road
Just might have to hard nose
Hard nose the highway
Hard nose the highway
Just might have to hard nose the highway
Hard nose the highway
Hard nose the highway
Further on

Further on
Further on up the road
I know you paid your dues in Canada
I know you paid your dues in Canada
But you just might
You just might have to hard nose
I hope not
I hope not
But you just might have to
I hope not
I hope not
But you just might have to hard nose
Hard nose the highway
Hard nose the highway

Wild Children

We were the war children
1945
When all the soldiers came marching home
Love looks in their eyes, in their eyes

Tennessee, Tennessee Williams
Let your inspiration flow
Let it be around while we hear the sound
Of the springtime rivers flow, rivers flow

Rod Steiger and Marlon Brando
Standing with their heads bowed on the side
Crying like a baby thinking about the time
James Dean took that fatal ride, took that ride

Tennessee Williams
Let your inspiration flow
Let it be around to hear the sound
When the springtime rivers flow, rivers flow

And Steiger and Marlon Brando
With their heads bowed on the side
Crying like a baby thinking about the time
James Dean took that fatal ride, took that ride

And we were the wild children
1945
When all the soldiers came marching home from war
With love looks, love looks in their eyes, in their eyes

The Great Deception

Did you ever hear about the great deception?
Well, the plastic revolutionaries take the money and run
Have you ever been down to Love City
Where they rip you off with a smile
And it don't take a gun?

Don't it hurt so bad in Love City
Don't it make you want to not bother at all?
And don't they look so self-righteous
When they pin you up against the wall?

Did you ever, ever see the people
With the teardrops in their eyes?
I just can't stand it, stand it no how
Living in this world of lies

Did you ever hear about the rock 'n' roll singers?
Got three or four Cadillacs
Saying, 'Power to the people, dance to the music'
Wants you to pat him on the back

Have you ever heard about the great Rembrandt?
Have you ever heard about how he could paint?
And he didn't have enough money for his brushes
And they thought it was rather quaint

But you know it's no use to heed it
And you know it's no use to think about it
'Cause when you start to think about it
You don't need it

Have you ever heard about the great
Hollywood motion-picture actor
Who knew more than they did?
And the newspapers didn't cover the story
Just decided to keep it hid

Somebody started saying it was an inside job
Whatever happened to him?
Last time they saw him down on the Bowery
With his lip hanging off an old rusty bottle of gin

Have you ever heard about the so-called hippies
Down on the far side of the track?
They take the eyeballs straight out of your head
Say, 'Son, kid, do you want your eyeballs back?'

Did you ever see the people
With the teardrops in their eyes?
Just can't stand it no how
Living in this world of lies

And did you ever hear about the great deception?
Well, the plastic revolutionaries take the money and run
Have you ever been down to Love City
Where they rob you with a smile
Instead of a gun?
Have you ever heard about
The great deception?

Bulbs

I'm kicking off from centrefield
A question of being down for the game
The one-shot deal don't matter
And the other one's the same

Oh my friend, I see you
Want you to come through
And they're standing in the shadows
Where the street lights all turn blue

She's leaving Pan-American
Suitcase in her hand
I said her brothers and her sisters
Are all on Atlantic sand

She's screaming through the alleyway
I hear the lonely cry, why can't you?
And her batteries are corroded
And her hundred-watt bulb just blew

La da da da da, da da da da da
La da da da da, da da da da da

She used to hang out down at Miss Lucy's
Every weekend they would get loose
Now Ada was a straight clear case of
Havin' taken in too much juice

It was outside, and it was outside
Just the nature of the person
Now all you got to remember
After all, it's all show biz

La da da da da, da da da da da
La da da da da, da da da da da

We're just screaming through the alleyway
I hear the lonely cry, ah why can't you?
And they're standing in the shadows
Canal Street lights all turn blue

And they're standing in the shadows
Where the street lights all turn blue
And they're standing in the shadows
Down where the street lights all turn blue

Comfort You

I wanna comfort you
I wanna comfort you
I wanna comfort you

Just let your tears run wild
Like when you were a child
I'll do what I can do
I wanna comfort you

You put the weight on me
You put the weight on me
You put the weight on me

When it gets too much for me
When it gets too much, much too much for me
I'll do the same thing that you do
And I'll put the weight on you

I'll put the weight on you
I'll put the weight on you
And I'll do the same thing that you do
I'll put the weight on you

I wanna comfort you
I wanna comfort you
And I wanna comfort you

Just let your tears run wild
Like when you were a child
I'll do what I can do
I just wanna comfort you

Come Here My Love

Come here, my love
This feeling has me spellbound
It's a storyline, in paragraphs laid down in song
In fathoms of my inner mind
I'm mystified, oh, by this mood
This melancholy feeling that just don't do no good

Come here, my love
And I will lift my spirits high for you
I'd like to fly away and spend a day or two
Just contemplating fields and leaves and talking about
  nothing
Just layin' down in shades of effervescent, effervescent odours
And shades of time and tide
And flowing through
Become enraptured by the sights and sounds and intrigue of
  nature's beauty
Come along with me
And take it all in
Come here, my love

Cul-de-Sac

In the cul-de-sac
Soft, clean eiderdown
Lay you down awhile
And take your rest

It's been much too long
Since you drifted into song
Relax yourself
And hide away

A trifle far
Nearest star
Mount Palomar
And we don't care who you know
It's what you are and who you are

And when they all go home
Down the cobblestones
You can double back
To a cul-de-sac
You can double back
To a cul-de-sac
You can double back
To a cul-de-sac

It Fills You Up

There's something going on
It fill you up, it fill you up, it fill you up now
There's something going on
It fill you up, it fill you up, it fill you up now

But you don't know what it is
But you don't know what it is
But you don't have to know
You just take it for what it is

Within this melody
It fill you up, it fill you up, it fill you up now
There's more than you can see
It fill you up, it fill you up, it fill you up now

There's another realm
There's another world
With kings and queens

That's why you got to testify
It fill you up, it fill you up, it fill you up now
You gotta do and die
It fill you up, it fill you up, it fill you up now

You got to stay on the music and move
You got to turn on the music and groove
Every, every, every day

You know what I'm talking about
It fill you up, it fill you up

It fill you up, it fill you up, it fill you up now
It fill you up, it fill you up, it fill you up now
It fill you up, it fill you up, it fill you up now
Get you rolling in the morning
It fill you up, it fill you up, it fill you up now
Work out a few kinks
It fill you up, it fill you up, it fill you up now
It fill you up to the brim, Jim
It fill you up, it fill you up, it fill you up now
Lord have mercy
It fill you up, it fill you up, it fill you up now
It fill you up, it fill you up, it fill you up now
Come here, baby
It fill you up, it fill you up, it fill you up now

Cold Wind in August

I waited for you
You waited for me
Well, it seemed like
Seemed like a mighty long time

Baby, I had to have you
You know I had to have you
Come rain, rain or shine
It was a cold wind in August
Shivers up and down my spine
I would stand in your garden
In the California pine

I was standin' shiverin'
I got the fever in the rain
But I kept coming back to see you
Again and again and again

I said I had to have you
Baby, I had to have you
Come rain, come rain or shine
It was a cold wind in August
Shivers up and down my spine
I would stand in your garden
In the California pine, California pine

It was a cold wind in August
Shivers up and down my spine
I would stand in your garden
In the California pine, in the California pine

It was a cold wind in August
I was pushed on through September
And I was pushin' through September in the rain
Pushin' through, pushin' through September in the rain

It was a cold wind in August
Shivers up and down my spine
I would stand, stand in your garden
In the California pine

Kingdom Hall

So glad to see you
So glad you're here
Come here beside me now
We can clear inhibition away
All inhibitions
Throw them away
And when we dance like this
We will dance like we've never before

Oh they were swingin'
Down at the Kingdom Hall
Oh bells were ringin'
Down at the Kingdom Hall
A choir was singin'
Down at the Kingdom Hall
They went
'Hey, liley, liley, liley,
Hey, liley, liley, low'

Good body music
Brings you right here
Free-flowin' motion now
When we're shakin' it out on the floor
Good rockin' music
Down in your shoes
And when we dance like this
Like we've never been dancin' before

They were swingin'
Down at the Kingdom Hall
Oh bells were ringin'

Down at the Kingdom Hall
A choir was singin'
Down at Kingdom Hall
They went
'Hey, liley, liley, liley,
Hey, liley, liley, low'

They were swingin'
Down at the Kingdom Hall
Bells were ringin'
Down at the Kingdom Hall
A choir was singin'
Down at the Kingdom Hall
They went
'Hey, liley, liley, liley,
Hey, liley, liley, low'

They were swingin'
Down at the Kingdom Hall
Oh bells were ringin'
Down at the Kingdom Hall
A choir was singin'
Down at the Kingdom Hall
They all went
'Hey, liley, liley, liley,
Hey, liley, liley, low

'Hey, liley, liley,
Hey, liley, low, low, low'
Down at the Kingdom Hall
Bells were ringin' out
And the choir was singin'
And the choir was singin'
'Hey, liley, liley,
Hey liley low, liley low, liley low,

Do do, do do, do do, do do'
Sugar was tough
Sugar was rough
Did you see Sugar?
Down at the Kingdom Hall
They were havin' a party
They were havin' a ball
And the people were dancin'
Down at the Kingdom Hall
Sugar was tough
Sugar was tough

Wavelength

This is a song about your wavelength
And my wavelength, baby
You turn me on
When you get me on your wavelength now
Yeah, yeah, yeah, yeah, yeah
With your wavelength
Oh with your wavelength
With your wavelength
With your wavelength
Oh mama, oh mama, oh mama
Oh mama, oh mama, oh mama, oh mama

Wavelength
Oh my, my
Wavelength
You never let me down, no, no
You never let me down, no, no

When I'm down you always comfort me
When I'm lonely, child, you see about me
You are everywhere you're supposed to be
And I can get your station
When I need rejuvenation

Wavelength
Oh my, my
Wavelength
You never let me down, no, no
You never let me down, no, no

I heard the Voice of America

Callin' on my wavelength
Tellin' me to tune in on my radio
I heard the Voice of America
Callin' on my wavelength
Singin', 'Come back, baby,
Come back,
Come back, baby
Come back'

Won't you sing that song again for me
About my lover, my lover in the grass?
You have told me 'bout my destiny
Singin', 'Come back, baby,
Come back,
Come back, baby,
Come back'

Wavelength
Oh my, my
Wavelength
You never let me down, no, no
You never let me down, no, no

When you get me on
When you get me on your wavelength
When you get me
Oh yeah, Lord
You get me on your wavelength

You got yourself a boy
When you get me on
Get me on your wavelength
Ya radio, ya radio, ya radio
Ya radio, ya radio, ya radio
Ya radio, ya radio, ya radio
Ya radio, ya radio, ya radio

Bright Side of the Road

From the dark end of the street
To the bright side of the road
We'll be lovers once again
On the bright side of the road

Little darlin', come with me
Won't you help me share my load
From the dark end of the street
To the bright side of the road?

And into this life we're born
Baby, sometimes, sometimes we don't know why
And time seems to go by so fast
In the twinkling of an eye

Let's enjoy it while we can
Won't you help me share my load
From the dark end of the street
To the bright side of the road?

And into this life we're born
Baby, sometimes, sometimes we don't know why
And it seems to go by so fast
In the twinkling of an eye

Let's enjoy it while we can
Help me sing my song
Little darlin', come alone
On the bright side of the road

From the dark end of the street

To the bright side of the road
Little darlin', come along
On the bright side of the road

From the dark end of the street
To the bright side of the road
We'll be lovers once again
On the bright side of the road

So we'll be lovers once again
On the bright side of the road

We'll be lovers once again
On the bright side of the road

Rolling Hills

Among the rolling hills
I'll live my life in Him
Well, I will live my life in Him
Among the rolling hills

And with my wife and child
I'll do no man no ill
Oh I will do no man no ill
Among the rolling hills

De de de de de de de de de
De de de de de de de de

Well, among the rolling hills
I read my Bible still
Oh I will read my Bible still
Among the rolling hills

With my pen I'll write my song
Among the rolling hills
With my pen I'll write my song
Among the rolling hills

De de de de de de de de de
De de de de de de de

And I will do my jig
Among the rolling hills
And I will do my jig and live
Among the rolling hills

With my pen I'll write my song
Among the rolling hills
With my pen I'll write my song
Among the rolling hills

And I'll stand and watch it all
Among the rolling hills
And I will stand and watch it all
Among the rolling hills

De de de de de de de de de
De de de de de

Take out my pen and write my song
Among the rolling hills
Take out my pen and write my song
Among the rolling hills
I'll take out my pen and write my song
Among the rolling hills

And the Healing Has Begun

And we'll walk down the avenue again
And we'll sing all the songs from way back when
And we'll walk down the avenue again
When the healing has begun

And we'll walk down the avenue in style
And we'll walk down the avenue and we'll smile
And we'll say, 'Baby, ain't it all worthwhile'
When the healing has begun

I want you to put on your pretty summer dress
You can wear your Easter bonnet and all the rest
And I wanna make love to you, yes, yes, yes
When the healing has begun
When the healing has begun

When you hear the music ringing in your soul
And you feel it in your heart and it grows and grows
And it came from the backstreet rock 'n' roll
When the healing has begun
That's where you come from, man

I want you to put on your, your old summer red dress
Put on your Easter bonnet and all the rest
And I wanna make love to you, yes, yes
When the healing has begun
I can't stand myself

We're gonna make music underneath the stars
We're gonna play to the violin and the two guitars
And we'll sit there for playing in hours

For hours, and hours, and hours, and hours, and hours
And hours, and hours, and hours
When the healing has begun
And hours, and hours, and hours, and hours
When the, when the healing has begun
Wait a minute

Listen, listen, listen, listen
I didn't know you stayed up so late
Ah you know I just got home from a, from a gig
I saw you standing on the street
Just let me move on up here
There's a windowsill a little bit here
Yeah, as I got some, dig some sherry, a drop of port
Yeah, I want you to come on in behind
Behind this door here
Why don't you just move on up this letterbox?
Why don't we just go in your front room and
Just sit down on the settee?
I'll just move on a little, a little bit now
Yeah, I gotta play this Muddy Waters record you got here
If you just open up a little bit there and just let me
Come on in, you know some backstreet jelly roll

We're gonna stay out all night long
And then we're gonna go out and roam across the fields
Baby, you know how I feel
When the healing has begun
When the healing, when the healing has begun
When the healing, when the healing has begun
We're gonna dance, we're gonna stay out all night long
We're gonna dance to the rock 'n' roll
When the healing has begun
Oh baby, now you just let me ease on a little bit
Dig this backstreet jelly roll

And the healing, and the healing has begun
And the healing has begun
And the healing, and the healing

You Know What They're Writing About

You know
You, you know what they're writing about
Baby, you, you know what they're talking about
Baby, you, you know what they're writing about
Baby, you know, you know what they're talking about

It's a thing called love
Down through the ages
It makes you wanna cry sometime
It makes you feel like you wanna lay down and die sometime
It make you high sometime
But when you really get in, in, in, in
It lifts you right up
You know what
You know what
You know what they're talking about
Baby, you, you, you, you, you, you, you, you, you know what
What they're writing about

It's a thing
It's a thing
It's love, baby

Ain't it a wonderful game?
Ain't it a wonderful, a marvellous game?

Ain't it a wonderful, ain't it a wonderful
Ain't it a wonderful game?
Yeah, when there's no more words to say about love, about love
It's all in the game, you know what they're talking about

Meet me down, meet me down
Meet me down by the river, baby
Meet me down, meet me down by the river

Meet me down, meet me down
Meet me by, by the water
Meet me down by the water
Baby, you know, I said you know what they're
You know what they're talking about

I want you to meet me, meet me down by the pylons
Meet me down by the pylons, meet me down by the pylons
Meet me down by the pylons

Meet me, I said meet me
I've got something I want to give to you
I've got something I want to give you
I want you to meet me
I want you to meet me
I want you to meet me

Are you there, I want you to meet me
Are you there, I want you to meet me
Are you there, are you there?
And you're there, and you're there
I want you to meet me
And no, no, no, no, no, no
And no, no, no
And no
And no, and no, no
And no
And no
I want you to meet
Are you, are you there?
I want you to be

Are you there?
I want you to meet me
Are you
Are you there, I want you to meet me
There
Are you there?
I want you to meet
Are you there, I want you to meet me
Are you there?
And no, no, no
And no, and no, and no
Are you there?
I want you to meet me

Summertime in England

Will you meet me in the country
In the summertime in England?
Will you meet me
Will you meet me in the country
In the summertime in England?
Will you meet me?
We'll go riding up to Kendal in the country
In the summertime in England
Did you ever hear about
Did you ever hear about
Did you ever hear about Wordsworth and Coleridge?
Did you ever hear about Wordsworth and Coleridge?
They were smokin' up in Kendal
By the lakeside

Can you meet me in the country in the long grass
In the summertime in England?
Will you meet me
With your red robe dangling all around your body
With your red robe dangling all around your body?
Will you meet me?
Did you ever hear about, did you ever hear about
Did you ever hear about, did you ever hear about
Did you ever hear about, did you ever hear about
William Blake
T. S. Eliot
In the summer
In the countryside?
They were smokin'
Summertime in England

Won't you meet me down by Bristol
Meet me along by Bristol?
We'll go riding down
Down by Avalon
Down by Avalon
Down by Avalon
In the countryside in England
With your red robe dangling, with your red robe dangling all around your body free
Let your red robe go
Go ridin' down by Avalon
Would you meet me in the country
In the summertime in England?
Would you meet me
In the church of St John
In the church of St John
In the church of St John
Down by Avalon
Down by Avalon
Down by Avalon
Down by Avalon?

Holy magnet
Give you attraction
I was attracted to you
Your coat was old, ragged and worn
And you wore it down through the ages
Ah the sufferin' did show in your eyes as we spoke
And the gospel music
The voice of Mahalia Jackson came through the ether

Oh my common one with the coat so old
And the light in the head
Said, Daddy, don't stroke me
Call me the common one

I said, oh the common one, my illuminated one
Oh my high-in-the-art-of-sufferin' one
Take a walk with me, take a walk with me down by Avalon
Oh my common one with the coat so old
And the light in the head
Keep the sufferin' so fine, and the sufferin' so fine
Take a walk with me down, down by Avalon
And I will show you it ain't why, why, why
It ain't why, why, why
It ain't why, why, why
It just is

Will you meet me in the country?
Will you meet me in the long grass down the country in the summertime?
Can you meet me in the long grass?
Wait a minute

With your red robe, with your red robe danglin'
All around your body
Yeats and Lady Gregory corresponded, corresponded
Corresponded, corresponded
And James Joyce wrote streams-of-consciousness books
Streams of
T. S. Eliot chose England, T. S. Eliot chose England
T. S. Eliot joined the ministry, joined the ministry, joined the ministry

Did you ever hear about, did you ever hear about
Wordsworth and Coleridge
Smokin' up in Kendal?
They were smokin' by the lakeside
Let your red robe go, let your red robe go
Let your red robe dangle in the countryside in England

We'll go ridin' down by Avalon in the country in the summertime in England
With you by my side
Let your red robe go, let your red robe go
You'll be happy dancin'
You'll be happy dancin'
You'll be happy dancin' in your red robe
Let it go, let it go, let it go, let your red robe go

Won't you meet me down by Avalon
In the summertime in England
In the church of St John
In the church of St John
In the church of St John
In the church of St John
In the church of St John?

Did you ever hear about Jesus walkin'
Jesus walkin' down by Avalon?
Can you feel the light in England?
Can you feel the light in England?
Can you feel the light in England?
Can you feel the light in England?

Oh my common one with the light in the head
And the coat so old
And the sufferin' so fine
Take a walk with me
Oh my common one, oh my illuminated one
Down by Avalon, down by Avalon
Oh my common one, oh my illuminated one
Oh my story time one
Oh my treasury in the sunset
Take a walk with me and I will show you

It ain't why, why, why, why
Why, why, why, why, why
Why, why, why, why, why
Why, why, why, why, why, why
It ain't why
It just is

It ain't why, why, why, why
Why, why, why, why, why
Why, why, why, why
It ain't why, why, why
It just is

It ain't why, why, why, why
Why, why, why
It just is

Oh my common one with the light in the head
And the coat so old
Oh my high-in-the-art-of-sufferin' one
Oh my high, oh my high, oh my high-in-the-art-of-sufferin' one
Oh my high-in-the-art-of-sufferin' one

Oh, my common one
Take a walk with me down by Avalon
And I will show you it ain't
It ain't why, why, why
It ain't why, why, why, why
It ain't why, it ain't why
It just is

Oh my common one with the light in the head
And the coat so fine
And the sufferin' is so high
Alright now

Oh my common one
Oh my common one
Oh my common one
Oh my common one
With the sufferin' so fine

It ain't why, why
It ain't why, why, why
It ain't why, why
It ain't why
It just is, that's all
It just is, that's all

Oh, oh my common one
With the coat so old and the light in the head
And the sufferin' and the sufferin' so fine
And the sufferin' so high

It ain't why
It ain't why
It ain't why
No, it ain't why
It just is, that's all about it
It just is
It just is, that's all there is to it
It just is, that's all there is about it
It just is, that's all there is to it
It just is, it just is

It just is right now
I want to go to church right now and say it just is
It just is, it just is

Oh my common one, my lovely headed one
Oh my high, oh my high-in-the-art-of-sufferin' one

It ain't why, why
It just is, that's all there is about it
Take a walk with me, talk with me
I will show you
It ain't why, it ain't why
It just is

Can you feel the light
Can you feel the light
Can you feel the light
Can you feel the light
Can you feel the light
Can you feel the light
Can you feel the light
Can you feel the light in your soul
In your soul, in your soul, in your soul, in your soul?
Ain't it high
Ain't it high
Ain't it high now

Oh my common one
Oh my story-time one
Oh my high-in-the-art-of-sufferin' one
Put your head on my shoulder
Put your head on my shoulder
And you listen, and you listen to the silence
Can you feel the silence?
Can you feel the silence?

Celtic Ray

When Llewellyn comes around
And he goes through market town
You'll be on the Celtic Ray
Are you ready?

When McManus comes around
On his early-morning round
Crying, 'Herring olay'
You'll be on the Celtic Ray

Ireland, Scotland, Brittany and Wales
I can hear those mothers' voices calling
'Children, children, children'

When the coal-brick man comes round
On a cold November day
You'll be on the Celtic Ray
Are you ready, are you ready?

Ireland, Scotland, Brittany and Wales
I can hear those mothers' voices calling
'Children, children, children'

Listen, Jimmy, I wanna go home
Listen, Jimmy, I wanna go home
I've been away from the Ray too long
I've been away from the Ray too long

All over Ireland, Scotland, Brittany and Wales
I can hear the mothers' voices calling
'Children, children, come home, children

Children, come home on the Celtic Ray'

In the early morning we'll go walkin'
Where the light comes shining through
On the Celtic Ray
Come on, children, come on, the Celtic Ray

Dweller on the Threshold

(Van Morrison and Hugh Murphy)

I'm a dweller on the threshold
And I'm waiting at the door
And I'm standing in the darkness
I don't want to wait no more

I have seen without perceiving
I have been another man
Let me pierce the realm of glamour
So I know just what I am

I'm a dweller on the threshold
And I'm waiting at the door
And I'm standing in the darkness
I don't want to wait no more

Feel the angel of the present
In the mighty crystal fire
Lift me up, consume my darkness
Let me travel even higher

I'm a dweller on the threshold
As I cross the burning ground
Let me go down to the water
Watch the great illusion drown

I'm a dweller on the threshold
And I'm waiting at the door
And I'm standing in the darkness
I don't want to wait no more

I'm gonna turn and face the music

The music of the spheres
Lift me up, consume my darkness
When the midnight disappears

I will walk out of the darkness
And I'll walk into the light
And I'll sing the song of ages
And the dawn will end the night

I'm a dweller on the threshold
And I'm waiting at the door
And I'm standing in the darkness
I don't want to wait no more

I'm a dweller on the threshold
And I cross the burning ground
And I'll go down to the water
Let the great illusion drown

I'm a dweller on the threshold
And I'm waiting at the door
And I'm standing in the darkness
I don't want to wait no more

I'm a dweller on the threshold
Dweller on the threshold
I'm a dweller on the threshold
I'm a dweller on the threshold

Beautiful Vision

Beautiful vision
Stay with me all of the time
Beautiful vision
Stay ever on my mind with your beautiful vision

Mystical rapture
I am in ecstasy
Beautiful vision
Don't ever separate me with your beautiful vision

In the darkest night
You are shining bright
You are my guiding light
You show me wrong from right

Beautiful vision
Stay ever on my mind
Beautiful vision
Stay with me all of the time with your beautiful vision

In the darkest night
You are shining bright
You are my guiding light
Show me wrong from right

Beautiful vision
Stay with me all of the time
Beautiful vision
Stay ever on my mind with your beautiful vision

I can make it
I can make it
With your beautiful vision

She Gives Me Religion

Down the mystic avenue I walk again
Remembering the days gone by
And I'm knocking with my heart
And all the girls walk by
In all their summer fashion
And the church bells chime
On a summer Sunday afternoon

She gives me religion
She gives me religion

And the angel of imagination
Opened up my gate
She said, 'Come right in,
I saw you knocking with your heart'

And the angel of imagination
Said, 'Lift your fiery vision bright,
Let your flame burn into the night,
I saw you knocking with your heart'

She gives me religion
She gives me religion

And all the girls walk by
In all their summer fashion
And the church bells chime
On a summer Sunday afternoon

She gives me religion
I said she gives me religion

And I'm knocking
And I'm knocking with my heart
And I'm knocking
Knocking with my heart
And I'm knocking with my heart

Cleaning Windows

Oh the smell of the bakery from across the street
Got in my nose
As we carried our ladders down the street
With the wrought-iron gate rows
I went home and listened to Jimmie Rodgers in my lunch
  break
Bought five Woodbine at the shop on the corner
And went straight back to work

Oh Sam was up on top
And I was on the bottom with the V
We went for lemonade and Paris buns
At the shop and broke for tea
I collected from the lady
And I cleaned the fanlight inside out
I was blowing saxophone on the weekend
In a Down joint

What's my line?
I'm happy cleaning windows
Take my time, I'll see you when my love grows
Baby, don't let it slide, I'm a working man in my prime
Cleaning windows
Number 36!

I heard Leadbelly and Blind Lemon
On the street where I was born
Sonny Terry, Brownie McGhee and
Muddy Waters singin' 'I'm a Rollin' Stone'
I went home and read my Christmas Humphreys book on
  Zen

Curiosity Killed the Cat
Kerouac's *Dharma Bums* and *On the Road*

What's my line?
I'm happy cleaning windows
Take my time, I'll see you when my love grows
Baby, don't let it slide, I'm a working man in my prime
Cleaning windows

What's my line?
I'm happy cleaning windows
Well, I take my time, I'll see you when my love grows
Don't let it slide, I'm a working man in my prime
Cleaning windows

Cleaning, what you sayin', number, number 126
Aye, we'll be round tomorrow
I just found a tanner and a 3d bit on the windowsill here
C'mon, Sammy, hurry up
If we don't get finished we'll have to go down to the dole
Cleaning windows

Higher Than the World

Well, I'm higher
Than the world
And I'm livin'
In my dreams
I'll make it better than it seems today

And I'm higher
Than a cloud
And I'm livin'
In a sound
I'll make it better than it seems today

Higher than the world
But my head is in a swirl
I got to give life a whirl today

Higher than the clouds
Wrapped up in a sound
I make it better all around today

Higher than the world
And my head is in a swirl
I got to give life a whirl today

Higher in my mind
I'm gonna leave these blues behind
And I'll find what I'll find today

'Cause I'm higher than the world
And I'm wrapped up in my dreams
I'll make it better than it seems today

Yes, I'm higher than the world
And I'm livin' in my mind
I got to hold on to what I find today
Just a little bit higher

River of Time

Heart and soul
Body and mind
Heart and soul
Body and mind
Heart and soul
Body and mind
Meet me on the river of time
Meet me on the river of time

Brother of mine
Sister of mine
Brother of mine
Sister of mine
Heart and soul
Body and mind
Meet me on the river of time
Meet me on the river of time

Lover of soul
Lover of mine
Lover of soul
Lover of mine
Heart and soul
Body and mind
Meet me on the river of time
Meet me on the river of time
Meet me on the river of time
On the river
River of time
On the river of time
On the river of time

Cry for Home

I'll be waiting
I'll be waiting on that shore
To hear the cry for home
You won't have to worry any more
When you hear the cry for home

When you hear, hear the call
You won't have to think at all
Hear the cry for home

I'll be standing
I'll be standing within reach
When you hear, hear the call
I'll be waiting
I'll be waiting in the breach
For you, when you hear

When you hear, hear the call
You won't have to think at all
Hear the cry for home

When I listen
When I listen to the song
Well, it feels, feels so free
And you tell me
You will come and go with me
When you hear the cry for home

When you hear, hear the call
You won't have to think at all
Hear the cry for home

When you hear, hear the call
You won't have to think at all
Hear the cry for home

When you hear, hear the call
You won't have to think at all
Hear the cry for home

Rave on, John Donne/Rave on, Part Two

Rave on, John Donne, rave on, thy holy fool
Down through the weeks of ages
In the moss-borne dark dank pools

Rave on down through the Industrial Revolution
Empiricism, the atomic and nuclear age
Rave on down through the corridors
Rave on words on printed page

Rave on, Walt Whitman, nose down in wet grass
Rave on, fill the senses
On nature's bright-green shady path

Rave on, Omar Khayyam, rave on, Khalil Gibran
Oh what sweet wine we drinketh
The celebration will be held
We will drink the wine and break the holy bread

Rave on, let a man come out of Ireland
Rave on, Mr Yeats, rave on down through thy holy Rosy Cross
Rave on down through Theosophy and the Golden Dawn
Rave on through the writing of *A Vision*
Rave on, rave on, rave on, rave on, rave on, rave on, rave on

Rave on, John Donne, rave on, thy holy fool
Down through the weeks of ages
In the moss-borne dark dank pools

Rave on down through the Industrial Revolution
Empiricism, and the atomic and nuclear age
Rave on words on printed page

Tonight 'neath the silvery moon, tonight
Tonight 'neath the silvery moon, tonight
And the leaves shake out of the trees
And the cool summer breeze
And the people passing in the street
And everybody that you meet

Tonight you will understand the oneness
Tonight you will understand the one
Tonight 'neath the silvery moon, tonight
Tonight, let it all begin, tonight
You will understand the oneness
The oneness, the oneness, the oneness, the oneness
The oneness, the oneness, the oneness

You made it real, what you sang about in your song
You made it real, what you sang about in your song
I said, 'Come back, baby, can we talk it over
One more time, tonight?'

Tonight you will understand the one, the oneness
Tonight 'neath the silvery moon, tonight
Tonight, let it all begin, tonight
You will understand the oneness
The oneness, the oneness, the oneness

And the truth what you sang about in your song
Oh baby, baby
And the truth what you sang about in your song
I said, 'No, no, no, no, no, no, no, no, no
No, no, no, no, no, no, no, no, no, no
No, no, no, no, no, no, no, no, no, no'

Tonight you will understand the one
Oh tonight you will under, understand the oneness

And the leaves shakin' on the trees
In the cool evening breeze
And the people passing in the street
And everybody that you meet
Tonight, tonight
When your lover's gone
Tonight, tonight

*

Tonight 'neath the silvery moon, tonight
Tonight 'neath the silvery moon, tonight
And the leaves shake out of the trees
And the cool summer breeze
And the people passing in the street
And everybody that you meet

Tonight you will understand the oneness
Tonight you will understand the one
Tonight 'neath the silvery moon, tonight
Tonight, let it all begin, tonight
You will understand the oneness
The oneness, the oneness, the oneness, the oneness
The oneness, the oneness, the oneness

You made it real, what you sang about in your song
You made it real, what you sang about in your song
I said, 'Come back, baby, can we talk it over
One more time, tonight?'

Tonight you will understand the one, the oneness
Tonight 'neath the silvery moon, tonight
Tonight, let it all begin, tonight
You will understand the oneness
The oneness, the oneness, the oneness

And the truth what you sang about in your song
Oh baby, baby
And the truth what you sang about in your song
I said, 'No, no, no, no, no, no, no, no, no
No, no, no, no, no, no, no, no, no, no
No, no, no, no, no, no, no, no, no, no'

Tonight you will understand the one
Oh tonight you will under, understand the oneness
And the leaves shakin' on the trees
In the cool evening breeze
And the people passing in the street
And everybody that you meet
Tonight, tonight
When your lover's gone
Tonight, tonight

Tore Down à la Rimbaud

Showed me pictures in the gallery
Showed me novels on the shelf
Put my hands across the table
Gave me knowledge of myself

Showed me visions, showed me nightmares
Gave me dreams that never end
Showed me light out of the tunnel
When there was darkness all around instead

I was just tore down à la Rimbaud
And I wish my message would come
Tore down à la Rimbaud
You know it's hard sometime
You know it's hard sometime

Showed me ways and means and motions
Showed me what it's like to be
Gave me days of deep devotion
Showed me things that I cannot see

Well, I was tore down à la Rimbaud
And I wish my purpose would come
Tore down à la Rimbaud
You know it's hard sometime
You know it's hard sometime

Showed me different shapes and colours
Showed me many different roads
Gave me very clear instructions
When I was in the dark night of the soul

When I was tore down à la Rimbaud
And I wish my writing would come
Tore down à la Rimbaud
You know it's hard sometime
You know it's hard sometime

Tore down à la Rimbaud
And I wish my writing would come
Tore down à la Rimbaud
You know it's hard sometime
You know it's hard sometime

Hard sometime
Tore down à la Rimbaud, à la Rimbaud
I was tore down à la Rimbaud, à la Rimbaud

Got to Go Back

When I was a young boy back in Orangefield
I used to look out my classroom window and dream
And then go home and listen to Ray sing
'I Believe to My Soul' after school
Ah that love that was within me
You know it carried me through
And it lifted me up and it filled me
Meditation, contemplation too

Got to go back
We've got to go back
Got to go back
Got to go back
For the healing
Go on with the dreaming

Ah there's people in the street
And the summer's almost here
Got to go outside in the fresh air
And walk while it's still clear
Breathe it in all the way down
To your stomach too
Breathe it out with a radiance
Into the night-time air

Got to go back
We've got to go back
Got to go back
Got to go back
For the healing
Go on with the dreaming

Got my ticket at the airport
Well, guess I've been marking time
I've been living in another country
That operates along entirely different lines
Keep me away from port or whiskey
Don't play anything sentimental it'll make me cry
Got to go now, my friend
Is there really any need to ask why?

Got to go back
Got to go back
Got to go back
We've got to go back
For the healing
Go on with the dreaming

We've got to go back
Baby, we've got to go back
Got to go back
Got to go back
For the healing
Go on with the dreaming

With the dreaming
With the dreaming
With the dreaming

In the Garden

The fields are always wet with rain
After a summer shower
When I saw you standing, standing in the garden
In the garden wet with rain

You wiped the teardrops from your eye in sorrow
As we watched the petals fall down to the ground
And as I sat beside you
I felt the great sadness that day
In the garden

And then one day you came back home
You were a creature all in rapture
You had the key to your soul and you did open
That day you came back
To the garden

The olden summer breeze was blowin' against your face
The light of God was shinin' on your countenance divine
And you were a violet colour
As you sat beside your father and your mother
In the garden

The summer breeze was blowin' on your face
Within your violet you treasure your summery words
And as the shiver from my neck down to my spine
Ignited me in daylight and nature
In the garden

And you went into a trance
Your childlike vision became so fine

And we heard the bells within the church we loved so much
And felt the presence of the youth of eternal summers
In the garden

And as it touched your cheeks so lightly
Born again you were and blushed
And we touched each other lightly
And we felt the presence of the Christ within our hearts
In the garden

And I turned to you and I said
'No guru, no method, no teacher,
Just you and I and nature and the Father
In the garden

'No guru, no method, no teacher,
Just you and I and nature
And the Father and the Son and the Holy Ghost
In the garden wet with rain

'No guru, no method, no teacher,
Just you and I and nature
And the Father and the Son and the Holy Ghost
In the garden,
In the garden wet with rain

'No guru, no method, no teacher,
Just you and I and nature and the Father
In the garden'

One Irish Rover

Tell me the story now
Now that it's over
Wrap it in glory
For one Irish Rover

Tell me you're wiser now
Tell me you're older
Wrap it in glory
For one Irish Rover

I can tell by the light in your eye
That you're so far away
Like a ship out on the sea without a sail
You've gone astray

Tell me the facts real straight
Don't make me over
Wrap it in glory
For one Irish Rover

Tell me you've seen the light
Tell me you know me
Make it come out alright
And wrap it in glory

For one Irish Rover
For one Irish Rover
For one Irish Rover
For one Irish Rover

Foreign Window

I saw you from a foreign window
Bearing down the suffering road
You were carrying your burden
To the palace of the Lord
To the palace of the Lord

I spied you from a foreign window
When the lilacs were in bloom
And the sun shone through your windowpane
To the place you kept your books
You were reading on your sofa
You were singing every prayer
That the masters had instilled in you
Since Lord Byron loved despair
In the palace of the Lord

And if you don't get it right this time
You don't have to come back again
And if you get it right this time
There's no need to explain

I saw you from a foreign window
Bearing down the suffering road
You were carrying your burden
You were singing about Rimbaud
I was going down to Geneva
When the kingdom had been found
I was giving you protection
From the loneliness of the crowd
In the palace of the Lord

They were giving you religion
Breaking bread and drinking wine
And you laid out on the green hills
Just like when you were a child
I saw you from a foreign window
You were trying to find your way back home
You were carrying your defects
Sleeping on a pallet on the floor
In the palace of the Lord
In the palace of the Lord
In the palace of the Lord

Tir Na Nog

We were standing in the kingdom
And by the mansion gate
We stood enraptured by the silence
As the birds sang their heavenly song
In Tir Na Nog

We stopped in the Church of Ireland
And prayed to Our Father
And climbed up the mountainside
With fire in our hearts
And we walked all the
Way to Tir Na Nog

I said with my eyes that
I recognised your chin
It was my long-lost friend
To help me from another lifetime
We took each other's hand and cried
Like a river when we said hello
And we walked all the way to Tir Na Nog

We made a big connection
On a golden autumn day
We were standing in the
Garden wet with rain
And our souls were young again
In Tir Na Nog

And outside the storm was raging
Outside Jerusalem
We drove in our chariots of fire

Following the sun in the west
Going up, going up to
Tir Na Nog

You came into my life
And you filled me and you filled me
Oh so joyous by the clear cool crystal streams
Where the roads were quiet and still
And we walked all the way
To Tir Na Nog

How can we not be attached?
After all we're only human
The only way then is to never come back
Except I wouldn't want that, would you
If we weren't together again
In Tir Na Nog

We've been together before
In a different incarnation
And we loved each other
Then as well
And we sat down in contemplation
Many, many, many times
You kissed mine eyes
In Tir Na Nog

I Forgot that Love Existed

I forgot that love existed, trouble in my mind
Heartache after heartache, worried all the time
I forgot that love existed
Then I saw the light
Everyone around me made everything alright

Oh Socrates and Plato
They praised it to the skies
Everyone who's ever loved
Everyone who's ever tried

If my heart could do the thinkin'
And my head begin to feel
Well, I'll look upon the world anew
And know what's truly real

Well, I forgot that love existed
And it strangled up my heart
Then I turned a brand-new leaf
And made a brand-new start

If my heart could do my thinkin'
And my head begin to feel
Well, I'd look upon the world anew
And know what's truly real

What's truly real
I forgot that love existed
And now it's alright
I forgot that love existed
And now it's alright

Someone Like You

I've been searching a long time
For someone exactly like you
I've been travelling all around the world
Waiting for you to come through
Someone like you; make it all worthwhile
Someone like you; keep me satisfied
Someone exactly like you

I've been travelling a hard road
Looking for someone exactly like you
I've been carrying my heavy load
Waiting for the light to come shining through
Someone like you; make it all worthwhile
Someone like you; make me satisfied
Someone exactly like you

I've been doing some soul-searching
To find out where you're at
I've been up and down the highway
In all kinds of foreign lands
Someone like you; make it all worthwhile
Someone like you; keep me satisfied
Someone exactly like you

I've been all around the world
Marching to the beat of a different drum
But just lately I have realised
The best is yet to come
Someone like you; make it all worthwhile
Someone like you; keep me satisfied
Someone exactly like you

Someone exactly like you
Someone exactly like you
The best is yet to come
The best is yet to come
Someone exactly like you

Alan Watts Blues

Well, I'm taking some time with my quiet friend
Well, I'm taking some time on my own
Well, I'm making some plans for my getaway
There'll be blue skies shining way up above

When I'm cloud-hidden
When I'm cloud-hidden
When I'm cloud-hidden
Whereabouts unknown

Well, I have to get out of the rat race now
Well, I'm tired of the ways of mice and men
And the empires are all turning into rust again
Out of everything nothing remains the same

That's why I'm cloud-hidden
Why I'm cloud-hidden
That's why I'm cloud-hidden
Whereabouts unknown

Sitting up on the mountain top
In my solitude
Where the fog comes rolling in
Just might do me some good

Well, I'm waiting in the clearing, with my motor on
Well, it's time to get back to the town again
Where the air is sweet and fresh in the countryside
Well, it won't be long before, be back here again

When I'm cloud-hidden

I'm cloud-hidden
When I'm cloud-hidden
Whereabouts unknown

I'm cloud-hidden
I'm cloud-hidden
When I'm cloud-hidden
Whereabouts unknown
Whereabouts unknown

Cloud-hidden
Cloud-hidden
Cloud-hidden
Whereabouts unknown

Did Ye Get Healed?

I wanna know did you get the feeling
Did you get it down in your soul?
I wanna know did you get the feeling
And did the feeling grow?

Sometimes when the spirit moves me
I can do many wondrous things
I wanna know when the spirit moves you
Did you get healed?

When I begin to realise it manifest in my life
In oh so many ways
Every day I wanna talk about it and walk about it
Every day I wanna be closer

I wanna know did you get the feeling?
Did you get it down in your soul?
I wanna know did you get the feeling?
Oh did you get healed?

When I begin to realise the magic in my life
See it manifest in oh so many ways
Every day it's getting better and better
I wanna be daily walking, daily walking close

It gets stronger when you get the feeling
When you get it down in your soul
And it make you feel good
And it make you feel whole

When the spirit moves you

And it fills you through and through
Every morning and at the break of day
Did you get healed?

Did you get healed?
Did you get healed?

Irish Heartbeat

Oh won't you stay, stay awhile
With your own ones?
Don't ever stray
Stray so far from your own ones
For the world is so cold
Don't care nothin' for your soul
You share with your own ones

Don't rush away, rush away
From your own ones
One more day, one more day
With your own ones
This old world is so cold
Don't care nothin' for your soul
You share with your own ones

There's a stranger
And he's standing by your door
Might be your best friend
Might be your brother
You may never know

I'm going back, going back
To my own ones
Back to talk, talk awhile
With my own ones
This old world is so cold
Don't care nothing for your soul
You share with your own ones

This old world is so cold
Don't care nothing for your soul
You share with your own ones

Whenever God Shines His Light

Whenever God shines His light on me
Open up my eyes so I can see
When I look up in the darkest night
I know everything's going to be alright

In deep confusion, in great despair
When I reach out for Him, He is there
When I am lonely as I can be
I know that God shines His light on me

Reach out for Him, He'll be there
With Him your troubles you can share
If you live the life you love
You get the blessing from above

He heals the sick and He heals the lame
Says you can do it too in Jesus's name
He'll lift you up and He turns you around
And puts your feet back on higher ground

Reach out for Him, He'll be there
With Him your troubles you can share
You can use His higher power
Every day and any hour

He heals the sick and He heals the lame
And He says you can heal them too in Jesus's name
He lifts you up and He turns you around
And puts your feet back on higher ground

Where He shines His light
Whenever God shines His light, on you, on you

He is the way, He is the truth, He is the light
Puts your feet back, puts your feet back
On higher ground, puts your feet back
Higher ground

Puts your feet back, puts your feet back
On higher ground, puts your feet back
On higher ground

Have I Told You Lately that I Love You?

Have I told you lately that I love you?
Have I told you there's no one above you?
Fill my heart with gladness
Take away my sadness
Ease my troubles, that's what you do

Oh the morning sun in all its glory
Greets the day with hope and comfort too
And you fill my life with laughter
You can make it better
Ease my troubles, that's what you do

There's a love that's divine
And it's yours and it's mine
Like the sun
At the end of the day
We should give thanks and pray to the One and say

Have I told you lately that I love you?
Have I told you there's no one above you?
Fill my heart with gladness
Take away my sadness
Ease my troubles, that's what you do

There's a love that's divine
And it's yours and it's mine
And it shines like the sun
At the end of the day
We will give thanks and pray to the One

Have I told you lately that I love you?

Have I told you there's no one above you?
Fill my heart with gladness
Take away my sadness
Ease my troubles, that's what you do

Take away my sadness
Fill my life with gladness
Ease my troubles, that's what you do

Fill my life with gladness
Take away my sadness
Ease my troubles, that's what you do

Coney Island

Coming back from Downpatrick
Stopping off at St John's Point
Out all day bird-watching
And the *craic* was good

Stopped off at Strangford Lough
Early in the morning
Drove through Shrigley taking pictures
And on to Killyleagh
Stopping for Sunday papers at the
Lecale district just before Coney Island

On and on, over the hill to Ardglass in the jam jar
Autumn sunshine, magnificent and all shining through
Stop off at Ardglass for a couple of jars of
Mussels and some potted herrings in case
We get famished before dinner

On and on, over the hill, and the *craic* is good
Heading towards Coney Island
I look at the side of your face
As the sunlight comes streaming through the window
In the autumn sunshine
And all the time going to Coney Island I'm thinking
'Wouldn't it be great if it was like this all the time?'

Orangefield

On a golden autumn day
You came my way in Orangefield
Saw you standing by the riverside in Orangefield
How I loved you then in Orangefield
Like I love you now in Orangefield

And the sun shone on your hair
When I saw you there in Orangefield
Saw you standing by the riverside in Orangefield
How I loved you then in Orangefield
Like I love you now in Orangefield

And the sun shone so bright
And it lit up all our days
You were the apple of my eye
Baby, it's true

On a golden autumn day
All my dreams came true in Orangefield
On a throne of Ulster day
You came my way in Orangefield
How I loved you then in Orangefield
Like I love you now in Orangefield

And the sun shone so bright
And it lit up all our lives
And the apple of my eye
Baby, was you

On a throne of Ulster day
You came my way in Orangefield

Saw you standing by the riverside in Orangefield
How I loved you then in Orangefield
Like I love you now in Orangefield

How I loved you then in Orangefield
Like I love you now in Orangefield

These Are the Days

These are the days of the endless summer
These are the days, the time is now
There is no past, there's only future
There's only here, there's only now

Oh your smiling face, your gracious presence
The fires of spring are kindling bright
Oh the radiant heart and the song of glory
Crying freedom in the night

These are the days by the sparkling river
His timely grace and our treasured find
This is the love of the one magician
Turned the water into wine

These are the days of the endless dancing
And the long walks on the summer night
These are the days of the true romancing
When I'm holding you oh so tight

These are the days by the sparkling river
And His timely grace and our treasured find
This is the love of the one great magician
Turned the water into wine

These are the days now that we must savour
And we must enjoy as we can
These are the days that will last for ever
You've got to hold them in your heart

So Quiet in Here

Foghorns blowing in the night
Salt sea air in the morning breeze
Driving cars all along the coastline
This must be what it's all about
Oh this must be what it's all about
This must be what paradise is like
So quiet in here, so peaceful in here
So quiet in here, so peaceful in here

The warm look of radiance on your face
And your heart beating close to mine
And the evening fading in the candle glow
This must be what it's all about
Oh this must be what it's all about
This must be what paradise is like
So quiet in here, so peaceful in here
So quiet in here, so peaceful in here

All my struggling in the world
And so many dreams that don't come true
Step back, put it all away
It don't matter, it don't matter any more
Oh this must be what paradise is like
This must be what paradise is like
It's so quiet in here, so peaceful in here
It's so quiet in here, so peaceful in here

A glass of wine with some friends
Talking into the wee hours of the dawn
Sit back and relax your mind
This must be, this must be, what it's all about

This must be what paradise is like
Oh this must be what paradise is like
So quiet in here, so peaceful in here
So quiet in here, so peaceful in here

Big ships out in the night
And we're floating across the waves
Sailing for some other shore
Where we can be what we wanna be
Oh this must be what paradise is like
This must be what paradise is like
Baby, it's so quiet in here, so peaceful in here
So quiet in here, peaceful in here
So quiet in here, so peaceful in here
So quiet in here, so quiet in here
So peaceful in here, so quiet in here

In the Days Before Rock 'n' Roll

(Van Morrison and Paul Durcan)

Justin, gentler than a man
I am down on my knees
At the wireless knobs
I am down on my knees
At those wireless knobs
Telefunken, Telefunken
And I'm searching for
Luxembourg, Luxembourg
Athlone, Budapest, AFN
Hilversum, Helvetia
In the days before rock 'n' roll

In the days before rock 'n' roll
In the days before rock 'n' roll
When we let, then we bet
On Lester Piggott when we met
We let the goldfish go
In the days before rock 'n' roll

Fats did not come in
Without those wireless knobs
Fats did not come in
Without those wireless knobs
Elvis did not come in
Without those wireless knobs
Nor Fats, nor Elvis
Nor Sonny, nor Lightnin'
Nor Muddy, nor John Lee

In the days before rock 'n' roll
In the days before rock 'n' roll

When we let and we bet
On Lester Piggott, ten to one
And we let the goldfish go
Down the stream
Before rock 'n' roll

We went over the wavebands
To get Luxembourg
Luxembourg and Athlone
AFN Stars of Jazz
Come in, come in, come in, Ray Charles
Come in, the high priest

In the days before rock 'n' roll
In the days before rock 'n' roll
When we let and we bet
On Lester Piggott, ten to one
And we let the goldfish go
And then The Killer came along, The Killer
The Killer, Jerry Lee Lewis
'A Whole Lotta Shakin' Goin' on'
'Great Balls of Fire'
Little Richard

Justin, gentler than a man
Justin, Justin, where is Justin now?
What's Justin doing now?
Just, where is Justin now?
Come aboard

Memories

Memories
All I have is memories
All I have is memories
Memories of you

Now you're gone
They linger on, these memories
All these precious memories
Memories of you

How they linger in the twilight
In the morning in the small hours
Just before dawn

Memories
Of summer days so long ago
People and the places
That we used to know
Oh those memories

How they linger in the twilight
And in the wee small hours
Sometimes just before the dawn

Oh those memories
Oh happy times, those memories
All I have now is memories
Memories of you

Oh memories
Oh those precious memories

All I have is memories
Memories of you

Memories of you
Memories of you
Oh those memories of you
Oh those memories of you
Oh the precious memories of you
Oh memories of you

Why Must I Always Explain?

Have to toe the line, I've got to make the most
Spent all these years going from pillar to post
Now I'm standing on the outside and I'm waitin' in the rain
Tell me why must I always explain?

Bared my soul to the crowd, but oh what the cost
Most of them laughed out loud like nothing's been lost
There were hypocrites and parasites and people that drain
Tell me why must I always explain?

Why, why must I always explain
Over and over, over again?
It's just a job you know and it's not 'Sweet Lorraine'
Tell me why must I always explain?

Well, I get up in the morning and I get my brief
I go out and stare at the world in complete disbelief
It's not righteous indignation that makes me complain
It's the fact that I always have to explain

I can't be everywhere at once, there's always somebody to see
And I never turned out to be the person that you wanted me
to be
And I tell you who I am time and time and time again
Tell me why must I always explain?

Well, it's out on the highway and it's on with the show
Always telling people things they're too lazy to know
It can make you crazy, it can drive you insane
Tell me why must I always explain?

See Me Through Part II (Just a Closer Walk with Thee)

Just a closer walk with Thee
Grant it, Jesus, if you please
I'll be satisfied as long as I walk, dear Lord, close to Thee

I am weak but Thou art strong
Jesus, keep me from all wrong
I'll be satisfied as long as I walk, dear Lord, close to Thee

See me through days of wine and roses
By and by when the morning comes
Jazz and blues and folk, poetry and jazz
Voice and music, music and no music
Silence and then voice
Music and writing, words
Memories, memories way back
Take me way back, Hyndford Street and Hank Williams
Louis Armstrong, Sidney Bechet on Sunday afternoons in winter
Sidney Bechet, Sunday afternoons in winter
And the tuning in of stations in Europe on the wireless
Before, yes, before this was the way it was
More silence, more breathing together
Not rushing, being
Before rock 'n' roll, before television
Previous, previous, previous
See me through, just a closer walk with Thee

Just a closer walk with Thee
Grant it, Jesus, if you please
I'll be satisfied as long as I walk, dear Lord, close to Thee

I am weak but Thou art strong
Jesus, keep me from all wrong
I'll be satisfied as long as I walk, dear Lord, close to Thee

Take Me Back

I've been walking by the river
I've been walking down by the water
I've been walking down by the river

I've been feeling so sad and blue
I've been thinking, I've been thinking, I've been thinking
I've been thinking, I've been thinking, I've been thinking
And there's so much suffering, and it's too much confusion
Too much, too much confusion in the world

Take me back, take me back, take me back
Take me way back, take me way back, take me way back
Take me way back, take me way back, take me way back
Take me way back, take me way back
Take me way, way, way, way, way, way, way back
Help me, help me understand
Take me, do you remember the time, darlin'
When everything made more sense in the world?
Oh I remember, I remember
When life made more sense
Ah take me back, take me back, take me back, take me back
Take me back, take me back, take me back, take me back
Take me back to when the world made more sense
Well, there's too much suffering and confusion
And I'm walking down by the river
Oh let me understand religion

Way back, way back
When you walked in a green field, in a green meadow
Down an avenue of trees
On a, on a golden summer

And the sky was blue
And you didn't have no worries, you didn't have no care
You were walking in a green field
In a meadow, through the buttercups, in the summertime
And you looked way out over, way out
Way out over the city and the water
And it felt so good and it felt so good
And you keep on walking

And the music on the radio and the music on the radio
Has so much soul, has so much soul
And you listen, in the night-time
While we're still and quiet
And you looked out on the water
And the big ships and the big boats
Came on sailing by, by, by, by
And you felt so good, and I felt so good
I felt I wanna blow my harmonica

Take me back there, take me way back
Take me back, take me back, take me back
Take me way, way, way back, way back
To when, when I understood
When I understood the light, when I understood the light
In the golden afternoon, in the golden afternoon
In the golden afternoon, in the golden afternoon
In the golden afternoons when we sat and listened to Sonny
   Boy blow

In the golden afternoon when we sat and let Sonny Boy blow,
   blow his harp

Take me back, take me back, take me back
Take me way, way, way, way, way, way, way
Back when I, when I understood, when I understood

Oh take me way back, when, when, when, when, when,
when
When, when, when, when, when, when, when
I was walking down the
Walking down the street in the rain
And it didn't matter
'Cause everything felt, everything felt, everything felt
Everything felt, everything felt, everything felt, everything felt
Everything felt, everything felt, everything felt so right

And so good
Everything felt so right, and so good
Everything felt so right, and so good
Everything felt so right, and so good
Everything felt so right, and so good
Everything felt so right, and so good, so good
In the eternal now, in the eternal moment
In the eternal now, in the eternal moment
In the eternal now
Everything felt so good, so good, so good, so good, so good
And so right, so right, so right, just
So good, so right, so right, in the eternal
In the eternal moment, in the eternal moment
In the eternal moment, in the eternal moment
When you lived, when you lived
When you lived in the light
When you lived in the grace
In the grace, in grace
When you lived in the light
In the light, in the grace
And the blessing

All Saints Day

Here comes Sue and she looks crazy
Skipping down the hillside daily
Looking like the flowers that bloom in May
Won't you make your reservation?
I will meet you at the station
Won't you come and see me, All Saints Day?

Follow the lead, it is no wonder, I seem to be so high
Living my dreams the way I ought to
As the days go rolling by

See me strolling through the meadow
With you, baby, by my side
Won't you come and see me, All Saints Day?

See the streamline blue horizon
With you, baby, by the way
Won't you come and see me, All Saints Day?
You can make your reservation
I will meet you at the station
When you come to see me, All Saints Day

When you come to see me, All Saints Day
When you come to see me, All Saints Day

Hymns to the Silence

Oh my dear, oh my dear sweet love
Oh my dear, oh my dear sweet love
When I'm away from you, when I'm away from you
Well, I feel, well, I feel so sad and blue
Well, I feel, well, I feel so sad and blue
Oh my dear, oh my dear, oh my dear sweet love
When I'm away from you, I just have to sing my hymns
Hymns to the silence, hymns to the silence
Hymns to the silence, hymns to the silence

Oh my dear, oh my dear sweet love, it's a long, long journey
Long, long journey, journey back home
Back home to you, feel you by my side
Long journey, journey, journey
In the midnight, in the midnight, I burn the candle
Burn the candle at both ends, burn the candle at both ends
Burn the candle at both ends, burn the candle at both ends
And I keep on, 'cause I can't sleep at night
Until the daylight comes through
And I just, and I just have to sing, sing my
Hymns to the silence, hymns to the silence
Hymns to the silence, my hymns to the silence

I wanna go out in the countryside
Oh sit by the clear cool crystal water
Get my spirit, way back to the feeling
Deep in my soul, I wanna feel
Oh so close to the one, close to the one
Close to the one, close to the one
And that's why I keep on singing, baby
My hymns to the silence, hymns to the silence

Oh my hymns to the silence, hymns to the silence
Oh hymns to the silence, oh hymns to the silence
Oh hymns to the silence, hymns to the silence
Oh my dear, my dear sweet love
Can you feel the silence, can you feel the silence?
Can you feel the silence, can you feel the silence?

Hymns to the silence, hymns to the silence
Hymns to the silence, hymns to the silence
Hymns to the silence, hymns to the silence
Hymns to the silence, hymns to the silence
Hymns to the silence, hymns to the silence

On Hyndford Street

Take me back, take me way, way, way back, on Hyndford Street
Where you could feel the silence at half past eleven on long summer nights
As the wireless played Radio Luxembourg and the voices whispered across Beechie River
In the quietness as we sank into restful slumber in the silence and carried on dreaming in God
And walks up Cherryvalley from North Road Bridge railway line on sunny summer afternoons
Picking apples from the side of the tracks that spilled over from the gardens of the houses on Cyprus Avenue
Watching the moth catcher work the floodlights in the evenings and meeting down by the pylons
Playing round Mrs Kelly's lamp, going out to Holywood on the bus
And walking from the end of the lines to the seaside, stopping at Fusco's for ice cream
In the days before rock 'n' roll
Hyndford Street, Abetta Parade, Orangefield, St Donard's Church
Sunday six bells and in between the silence there was conversation
And laughter and music and singing and shivers up the back of the neck
And tuning into Luxembourg late at night and jazz and blues records during the day
Also Debussy on the Third Programme, early mornings when contemplation was best
Going up the Castlereagh Hills and the Cregagh Glens in summer and coming back

To Hyndford Street, feeling wondrous and lit up inside, with
a sense of everlasting life
And reading Mr Jelly Roll and Big Bill Broonzy and *Really
the Blues* by Mezz Mezzrow
And *Dharma Bums* by Jack Kerouac, over and over again
And voices echoing late at night over Beechie River
And it's always being now, and it's always being now
It's always now. Can you feel the silence?
On Hyndford Street where you could feel the silence
At half past eleven on long summer nights
As the wireless played Radio Luxembourg and the voices
whispered across Beechie River
And in the quietness we sank into restful slumber in silence
And carried on dreaming in God

Too Long in Exile

Too long in exile
Too long not singing my song
Too long in exile
Too long like a rolling stone
Too long in exile

Too long in exile
Baby, those people just ain't, just ain't your friends
Too long in exile, my friend
You can never go home again

Well, that isolated feeling
Drives you so close up against the wall
Till you feel like you can't go on
You've been in the same place for too long

Too long in exile
Baby, you can never go back home
Too long in exile
Any way you want

Oh that isolated feeling
Drives you up against, up against the wall
'Cause you've been on the mainland, baby
Been on the mainland, comin' on strong

Too long in exile
Too long people keep hanging on
Too long in exile
Too long like a rolling stone

And the wheeling and the dealing
All takes up too much time
Check your better self, baby
You'd better satisfy, satisfy your mind

Too long in exile
Too long you've been grinding at the mill
Too long in exile
Man, I've really just had my fill

Too long in exile
You can never go back home again
Too long in exile
Just about to drive me just insane

Too long in exile, been too long in exile
Just like James Joyce, baby
Too long in exile
Just like Samuel Beckett, baby
Too long in exile
Just like Oscar Wilde
Too long in exile
Just like George Best, baby
Too long in exile
Just like Alex Higgins, baby
Too long in exile

Wasted Years
(duet with John Lee Hooker)

Wasted years being brainwashed by lies
 Oh yes I have
Oh wasted years
 I'm talking about wasted years
Oh I'm not seeing eye to eye
 I just can't see the things I should see
Wasted years, baby
I was taking the wrong advice
 I know you was, I know you was
 And I was too

All alone I'm travelling
Travelling through these wasted years
 For so long, so long, so long I was
Oh I must have gained some wisdom
 Down through the years I did
Somewhere along the way
 Oh yes I did, oh yes I did
That's why there can't be no more
 No more
No more wasted years today
 I got wise, I got wise to myself

Well, baby, the great sadness
Oh you've got to let it all go
 Oh yeah, oh yeah, Van
Live in the present
Live in the future, Johnny, ain't that so?
 Oh it's a sad feeling, oh yeah
Oh you've gotta find something

To carry you through, carry you through
Carry you through

I've learned my lesson
I ain't gonna do it no more, yeah
Now, Van
Now, John
I've learned my lesson
I should have a long time ago
That's right
All these wasted years, wasted years
I finally woke up and got wise
I ain't gonna be, ain't gonna be no fool no more
Now, Van, now, Van
Ain't gonna be nobody's, 'body's fool no more
Sing the song, Van, sing it with me

Well, all alone, all alone I've been travelling
Travelling all alone through these wasted years
Dark, dark wasted years
So dark here
Dark, dark, dark, dark wasted years
I must have gained something
Oh travelling along the lonely way
Yeah, I've learned a lesson
I'm gonna make damn sure, baby, make damn sure
There's no more wasted years today

No Religion

We didn't know no better and they said it could be worse
Some people thought it was a blessing
Other people think that it's a curse
It's a choice between fact and fiction
And the whole world has gone astray
That's why there's no religion, no religion, no religion here
today

And there's no straight answers
Of what this thing called love is all about
Some say it's unconditional
Other people just remain in doubt
When I cleaned up my diction, I had nothing left to say
Except there's no religion, no religion, no religion here today

And they ask what hate is, it's just the other side of love
Some people want to give their enemies
Everything they think that they deserve
Some say, 'Why don't you love your neighbour?
Go ahead and turn the other cheek'
But there's nobody on this planet that can ever be so meek
And I can't bleed for you, you have to do it your own way
And there's no religion, no religion, no religion here today

No religion, no religion, no religion here today

And they ask what hate is, it's the other side of love
Some people want to give their enemies
Everything they think that they deserve
Others say, 'Why don't you love your neighbour?
Go ahead and turn the other cheek'

Have you ever met anybody who'd ever been that meek?
And it's so cruel to expect the Saviour to save the day
And there's no religion, no religion, no religion here today

And there's no mystery and there's nothin' hidden
And there's no religion here today

And there's no mystery and there's nothin hidden
And there's no religion here today

And there's no religion, no religion, no religion here today

Songwriter

I'm a songwriter and I know just where I stand
I'm a songwriter, pen and paper in my hand
Get the words on the page
Please don't call me a sage
I'm a songwriter

I'm a songwriter and I do it for a living
I'm a songwriter and I write about men and women
I can write about love and the stars up above
I'm a songwriter

I'm a songwriter and I'm hot on your trail
I'm a songwriter and my cheque's in the mail
I can move with the scene, I can make up a dream
I'm a songwriter

I'm a songwriter, I can do it for certain
I'm a songwriter, even do it when I'm hurtin'
And if it comes to the bit, have to write another hit
I'm a songwriter

I'm a songwriter, I can put it in words
I'm a songwriter and it's not for the birds
I can spin you a yarn, it's as long as my arm
I'm a songwriter

I'm a songwriter
I'm a songwriter

Days Like This

When it's not always raining, there'll be days like this
When there's no one complaining, there'll be days like this
When everything falls into place like the flick of a switch
Well, my mama told me, there'll be days like this

When you don't need to worry, there'll be days like this
When no one's in a hurry, there'll be days like this
When you don't get betrayed by that old Judas kiss
Oh my mama told me, there'll be days like this

When you don't need an answer, there'll be days like this
When you don't meet a chancer, there'll be days like this
When all the parts of the puzzle start to look like they fit
Then I must remember, there'll be days like this

When everyone is upfront and they're not playing tricks
When you don't have no freeloaders out to get their kicks
When it's nobody's business the way that you wanna live
I just have to remember, there'll be days like this

When no one steps on my dreams, there'll be days like this
When people understand what I mean, there'll be days like this
When you ring out the changes of how everything is
Well, my mama told me, there'll be days like this

Oh my mama told me, there'll be days like this
Oh my mama told me, there'll be days like this
Oh my mama told me, there'll be days like this

Fire in the Belly

Call of the wildest, it's got the best of you
I got fire in my heart, fire in my belly too
Got a heart and a mind and a fire inside
And I'm crazy about you
You, you on your high-flying cloud
You, you when you're laughing out loud
You, you with your hidden surprise
You

Stoke up my engine, bring me my driving wheel
Once I get started, you'll know just how I feel
And I'm crazy about you
And I'm crazy about you
And I'm crazy about you
You, you on your high-flying cloud
You, you when you're laughing out loud
You, you with your hidden surprise
You

Gotta get through January
Gotta get through February
Gotta get through January
Gotta get through February
Gotta get through January
Gotta get through February
Gotta get through January

Spring in my heart, fire in my belly too
I come apart, I don't know just what to do
Got a heart and a mind and a fire inside
And I'm crazy about you

You, you on your high-flying cloud
You, you with the laugh in your eyes
You, you with your hidden surprise
You

Gotta get through January
Gotta get through February
Gotta get through January
Gotta get through February
Gotta get through January
Gotta get through February
Gotta get through January

Spring in my heart, fire in my belly too
I come apart, I don't know just what to do
I got a heart and a mind and a fire inside
And I'm crazy about you
You, you on your high-flying cloud
You, you with the laugh in your eyes
You, you with your hidden surprise
You

Talkin' 'bout you
Talkin' 'bout you
Talkin' 'bout you
Talkin' 'bout you
Talkin' 'bout you
Talkin' 'bout you, talkin' 'bout you
Talkin' 'bout you, fire in the belly too

Talkin' 'bout you, talkin' 'bout you
Talkin' 'bout you, talkin' 'bout you
Talkin' 'bout you, talkin' 'bout you
Talkin' 'bout you, talkin' 'bout you
Talkin' 'bout you, talkin' 'bout you
Talkin' 'bout you

Burning Ground

And I take you down to the burning ground
And you change me up and you turn it around
In the wind and rain I'm gonna see you again
In the morning sun and when the day is done
And you take my hand and you walk with me
And sometimes it feels like eternity
And I turn the tide, I get back my pride
And I make you proud when you say it out loud
When I you take you down to the burning ground
To the burning ground, to the burning ground
To the burning ground, to the burning ground

And I take you down by the factory
And I show you like it has to be
And you understand how the work is done
And I pick up the sack in the midday sun
And I pull you through by the skin of your teeth
And I lift the veil to see what's underneath
And you return to me and you sit on your throne
And you make me feel that I'm not alone
And I take you down to the burning ground
To the burning ground, to the burning ground
To the burning ground

Hey, man, who's that you're carrying?

Feels like lead

It weighs a ton – let's see if we can dump it by the side of the hill

Hey, wait up, why don't you dump it on the burning ground?

Dump it down there

Yeah, man, dump the jute

Hey, man, dump the jute on the burning ground

Dump the jute?

Yeah, you know, dump the jute

Dump the jute!

On the burning ground
On the burning ground

And you make me think what it's all about
Sometimes I know, gonna work it out
And I watch you run in the crimson sun
Tear my shirt apart, open up my heart
And I watch you run down on your bended knees
By the burnt-out well, can you tell me please?
Between heaven and hell won't you take me down
To the burning ground, to the burning ground
To the burning ground, to the burning ground?

And you fall and pray, when you hear that sound
And we're walking back to the burial mound
And you shake your head and you turn it around
And you see the flames from the burning ground
And you get down on your knees and pray
And I catch my breath as we're running away
And I take the jute and I throw him down
On the burning ground, on the burning ground
On the burning ground, it's on the burning ground

Sometimes We Cry

Sometimes we know, sometimes we don't
Sometimes we give, sometimes we won't
Sometimes we're strong, sometimes we're wrong
Sometimes we cry

Sometimes it's bad when the going gets tough
Yet we look in the mirror and we want to give up
Sometimes we don't even think we'll try
Sometimes we cry

Well, we're gonna have to sit down and think it right through
If we're only human what more can we do?
The only thing to do is eat humble pie
Sometimes we cry

'Fore they put me in a jacket and they take me away
I'm not gonna fake it like Johnnie Ray
Sometimes we live, sometimes we die
Sometimes we cry

Sometimes we can't see anything straight
Sometimes everybody is on the make
Sometimes it's lonely on the lost highway
Sometimes we cry, sometimes we cry

Gonna put me in a jacket and take me away
I'm not gonna fake it like Johnnie Ray
Sometimes we live, sometimes we die
Sometimes we cry, sometimes we cry

Sometimes we live, sometimes we die
Sometimes we cry, sometimes we cry

Not Supposed to Break Down

You're not supposed to be human
You're not supposed to really feel
Not supposed to get involved with
Anything completely real
Fifteen families starving
All around the corner block
Here we're standing so alone
Just like Gibraltar Rock

Not supposed to break down
You're not supposed to break down
Swallow the dirt
Keep listening to the hurt
You'll be safe and sound

Supposed to be superhuman
Cover everything
Just like a bird
Cover an egg with its wing
And you know there's nothing sacred
But what is the use?
No point trying to find
What it's worth, what is true

Not supposed to break down
You're not supposed to break down
Swallow the hurt
Listen to the dirt
You'll be safe and sound

You're not supposed to break down

You're not supposed to break down
Swallow the hurt
Listen to the dirt
You'll be safe and sound

A fool and his mainline connection
Bypass going to the well
But that doesn't matter any more
I'm sure that we can tell
Who's a puppet on a string
And who really holds the glove
But it ain't up to you and me
It's up to the Lord above

You're not supposed to break down
You're not supposed to break down
Swallow the hurt
Keep on listening to the dirt
And I'll bet you'll be safe and sound

You're not supposed to break down
You're not supposed to break down
Swallow the hurt
Listen to the dirt
I'll bet you'll be safe and sound
And I'll bet you'll be safe and sound
And I'll bet you'll be safe and sound
I'll bet you'll be safe and sound

Madame Joy

All the men would turn their head
When she walked down the street
Clothes were fine and hair that shines
Smiling oh so sweet, smiling oh so sweet

Got a taste of old religion
Comes on with the new
In her hair a yellow ribbon
And she's decked out all in blue
Oh yes in, decked out all in blue

Steppin' lightly, steppin' brightly
With her books in hand
Going to the university to teach and
Help them understand
And help them understand

And all the kids would love to see her
Follow in her steps
And tell her stories and adore her
Climb in through the fence
Climb in through the fence

Here she comes walking
Here she comes talking
I do believe it's Madame Joy
Walking past that old street corner
And she's looking for her boy
Oh yes she is, looking for her boy

Steppin' lightly, steppin' brightly

With her books in hand
Going to the university to teach and
Help them understand
Help them understand

I was looking at the way she moved me
And I was seeing every sign
Tell me, can I learn the language?
Have you got the mind?
Have you got the mind?

Here she comes walking
Here she comes talking
I do believe it's Madame Joy
She's walking by that old street corner
And she's looking for her boy
Looking for her boy

And all the men would turn their head
When she walked down the street
Clothes refined and hair that shines
And smiling oh so sweet, oh yes, she's smiling oh so sweet
Smiling, smiling oh so sweet
Smiling, smiling oh so sweet

And all the men would
And all the men would turn their head around
When that woman walked down the street
When that woman walked down the street
When that, when that woman walked
When that woman walked, when that woman walked
When that woman walked, when that woman walked
When that woman walked, what she wore
When that woman, when that woman, when that woman
When that woman, when that woman, when that woman

When that woman, when that woman, when that woman
When that woman, when that woman walked
She just walked
Just kept on walking down the street
When she walked, when she walked down
When she walked on down

Naked in the Jungle

Naked in the jungle, naked to the world
Naked in the jungle, naked to the world
Well, you gotta keep it humble, else it'll come unfurled

Lions and the tigers, grazin' in the grass
Lions and the tigers, grazin' in the grass
There's a keeper watching over, make sure no one gets past

Speak out, speak out, speak out, speak out
Speak out, speak out, speak out, speak out
Speak out, speak out, speak out, speak out
Speak out, speak out, speak out, speak out

Big fish eat the little fish and the rabbit's on the run
Big fish eat the little fish and the rabbit's on the run
Some folks gettin' too much, others just ain't gettin' none

Naked in the jungle, naked to the world
Naked in the jungle, naked to the world
Well you gotta keep it humble, else it'll come unfurled

Let's go, boy
Speak out, speak out, speak out, speak out
Speak out, speak out, speak out, speak out
Speak out, speak out, speak out, speak out
Speak out, speak out, speak out, speak out

The Street Only Knew Your Name

Your street, rich street or poor
You should always be sure of your street
There's a place in your heart, when you know from the start
And you can't be complete without a street

Keep movin' on, just like a train
Sometimes you gotta look back to the street again
Would you prefer all those castles in Spain
Or a view of the street from your windowpane?

When you were young, so young
So very, very young
When you were young, so young
So very, very, very young
And the street only knew your name
And the street only knew your name
And the street only knew your name, oh your precious name,
 precious name

There was Walter and John, Katie and Ron
They all hung around the corner lamplight
Get together, sing some songs
Like 'Boppin' the Blues'
'You Make Me Feel Alright'

That was long before fortune and fame
No such thing as a star when you played that game
Everyone knew who everyone was
There was no pretence in the street, no, no

When you were young, so young

So very, very, very, very young
When you were young, so young
So very, very, very young
And the street only knew your name
And the street only knew your name
And the street only knew your name, oh your name, your
  precious name

And you walked around in the heart of town
Listening for that sound
And you walked around in the heart of town
Listening for that sound
'Blue Suede Shoes', it was the 'Blue Suede Shoes'

When you were young, so young
So very, very, very, very young
When you were young, so young
Very, very, very young
And the street only knew your name
And the street only knew your name
And the street only knew your name
Talking 'bout the street now, baby

We were singing 'Be-Bop-A-Lula'
We were singing 'Blue Suede Shoes'
We were singing 'Good Golly Miss Molly'
We were singing 'Tutti Frutti'
We were singing 'What'd I Say'
We were singing 'Boppin' the Blues' and 'Who Slapped John?'
When the street only knew your name
Talkin' about a funky street now, baby

And the street only knew your name

Show Business

Say you wanna be in show business
See the man on the TV with a phoney smile
Bring you up, bring you down
He can turn your head around
In show business, show business

See the man on a silver screen
With the phoney smile
Bring you up, bring you down
He can turn your head around
Show business, show business

Have a hit, maybe two
Make mincemeat out of you
Come back in two years' time
Lay your heart right on the line
In show business, show business
Show business, show business

Where's the next one, where's the next one?
Where's the next one?
Oh baby, just like the last one
Like the last one

Say you wanna be in show business
See the man in the suit
With the phoney smile
He can laugh, he can cry
He can make you reach the sky
He can say anything you wanna hear
Be anything you wanna be

He can say anything you want to hear
Be anything you want him to be
Make you leave your family
In show business, in show business

Take it to the bridge
And the next one and the next one
And the next one
Can you do it like the last one?
Now do it just like the last one, please
Like the last one, like the last one
Just like the last one

Say you wanna be in show business
Have a pretty face and a pretty smile
I'm thinking
Make you laugh and they can make you cry
But they can't wait, wipe the teardrops from your eye
In show business, show business

Say you wanna be in show business
See the rock star up on the stage
Right now
Behind them drugs, behind them booze
Behind them people he can use
Behind them people usin' them
Behind them people usin' us
And the next one and the next one
And the next one
Can you make it just like the last one?
Oh you make it just like the last one
Like the last one
Just like the last one

Say you wanna be in show business

All the world is a stage
Everybody must play their part
I've been so long in show business
I feel right now just like I got myself a start
Forget the junk, forget the jive
I just want to stay alive
In show business, in show business

Take it to the bridge
And the next one and the next one
And the next one
Oh just like the last one, just like the last one
Like the last one

Can I rob you with a fountain pen?
But you got to find some honest men
They can make you leave your home
Where you go to waste and roam
Control your fate, control your life
They can make you leave your wife
It's show business, it's show business

Take it to the bridge
And the next one and the next one
And the next one
Oh just like the last one
Can you make it
Like the last one?
Can you give it one more time
Like the last one?
Can you put it out like the last one?
Show business, it's show business
It's show business, show business
It's show business, show business
It's show business, show business

Philosopher's Stone

Out on the highways and the byways all alone
I'm still searching for, searching for my home
Up in the morning, up in the morning out on the road
And my head is aching and my hands are cold
And I'm looking for the silver lining, silver lining in the
   clouds
And I'm searching for
And I'm searching for the philosopher's stone

And it's a hard road, it's a hard road, daddy-o
When my job is turning lead into gold
He was born in the backstreet, born in the backstreet Jelly
   Roll
I'm on the road again and I'm searching for
The philosopher's stone
Can you hear that engine?
Oh can you hear that engine drone?
Well, I'm on the road again and I'm searching for
Searching for the philosopher's stone

Up in the morning, up in the morning
When the streets are white with snow
It's a hard road, it's a hard road, daddy-o
Up in the morning, up in the morning
Out on the job
Well, you've got me searching for
Searching for, the philosopher's stone
Even my best friends, even my best friends they don't know
That my job is turning lead into gold
When you hear that engine, when you hear that engine
   drone

I'm on the road again and I'm searching for the philosopher's
stone

It's a hard road, even my best friends they don't know
And I'm searching for, searching for the philosopher's stone

High Summer

By the mansion on the hillside
A red sports car comes driving down the road
And pulls up into the driveway
And the story does unfold

She's standing by the rhododendrons
Where the roses are in bloom
Looking out at the Atlantic Ocean
And in her head she hums this tune

Thank God the dark nights are drawing in again
'Cause high summer has got me down
Have to wait till the end of August
And to get off this merry-go-round

And they shut him out of paradise
Called him Lucifer and frowned
'Cause he took pride in what God made him
Even before the angels shot him down to the ground

He's a light out of the darkness
And he wears a starry crown
If you see him, nothin's shakin'
'Cause high summer has got him low down

High summer's got him lonesome
Even when he makes the rounds
There's been no two ways about it
High summer's got him low down

Checked into the tiny village by the lakeside

Settled down to start anew
Far away from the politicians
And the many chosen few

Far away from the jealousy factor
And everything that was tearing him apart
Far away from the organ grinder
And everyone that played their part

And they shut him out of paradise
Called him Lucifer and frowned
'Cause he took pride in what God made him
Even before the angels shot him to the ground

He's a light out of the darkness
And he wears a starry crown
If you see him nothin's shakin'
High summer's got him low down

High summer's on the rebound
High summer's got him low down
High summer's on the rebound
High summer's got him low down
High summer's on the rebound
High summer's got him low down
Low down

Choppin' Wood

You wired the trains and went back home to St Clair Shores
Before you became a spark down at the yard
You were passing through those hungry years alone
You were just trying to make a living out in Detroit

When you came back off the boats you didn't want to go anywhere
You sit down to TV in your favourite chair
You watched the big picture fade away down at Harland and Wolff
But you still kept on choppin' wood

And you came back home to Belfast
So you could be with us *like*
You lived a life of quiet desperation on the side
Going to the shipyard in the morning on your bike

Well, the spark was gone but you carried on
You always did the best you could
You sent for us once but everything fell through
But you still kept on choppin' wood, choppin' wood

Well, you came back home to Belfast
So you could be with us *like*
And you lived a life of quiet desperation on the side
Going to the shipyard in the morning on your bike

Well, the spark was gone but you carried on
Well, you did just the best that you could
You sent for us one time but everything fell through
But you still kept on choppin' wood

Kept on choppin' wood
Kept on choppin' wood
Local man chops wood
You know you did the best you could

Well, everything just fell through
Kept on choppin' wood
Chop, chop, chop, chop, chop
Chop, chop, chop, chop, chop
Chop, chop, chop, keep on choppin'
Chop, chop, chop, choppin' wood

What Makes the Irish Heart Beat

All that trouble, all that grief
That's why I had to leave
Staying away too long is in defeat
Why I'm singing this song
When I'm heading back home
That's what makes the Irish heart beat

I'm just like a hobo riding a train
I'm like a gangster living in Spain
Have to watch my back and I'm running out of time
Well, I'll roll the dice again
If Lady Luck will call my name
That's what makes the Irish heart beat

Well, that's what makes it beat
When I'm standing on the street
And I'm standing underneath this Wrigley's sign
Oh so far away from home
But I know I've got to roam
That's what makes the Irish heart beat

And it was off to foreign climes
On the Piccadilly line
We were standing underneath the Wrigley's sign
So far away from home
Well, I know I've got to roam
That's what makes the Irish heart beat

Just like a sailor out on the foam
Any port in a storm
When we tend to burn the candle at both ends

Down the corridors of fame
Like the spark ignites the flame
That's what makes the Irish heart beat

But I'll roll the dice again
If Lady Luck will call my name
That's what makes the Irish heart beat
Oh that's what makes the Irish heart beat
That's what makes the Irish heart beat

What's Wrong with This Picture?

What's wrong with this picture?
There's something I'm not seeing here
What's wrong with this picture?
Something's not exactly clear

What's wrong with this picture?
Does it look like it's just another sting, sting?
'Cause it don't mean a thing
If it ain't got that swing and ring a ding ding

What's wrong with this picture?
Doesn't anybody see
That's who everyone thought
That I used to be?

What's wrong with this picture?
It's only just hanging on a wall
So you can go right back to sleep
And just forget about it all, because

I'm not that person any more
I'm living in the present time
Baby, don't you understand
I've left all that jive behind

You can't believe what you read in the papers
Or half the news that's on TV
Or the gossip of the neighbours
Or anyone who doesn't want you to be free

I'm not that person any more

I'm always living in the present time
Don't you understand?
I left all that jive behind

What's wrong with this picture?
It's only hanging on the wall
Why don't we take it down and
Just forget about it 'cause that ain't me at all?

Somerset

We met deep down in Somerset
A time I can't forget
When we were sippin' cider in the shade

Oh the sun was setting in the west
You looked your very best that night
Stars were shining in your eyes

And we walked, walked all along the sand
And it felt, felt like a wonderland

And when the summer breeze was gone
The memory lingered on
You and me down in Somerset

Oh we walked, walked and walked and walked all along the sand
And it felt just like our love just began

And when the summer breeze was gone
The memory lingered on, me and you
When the summer set

We met, we met, we met deep down in Somerset
A time I can't forget
You were sippin' cider in the shade

Meaning of Loneliness

Lost in a strange city, nowhere to turn
Far cry from the streets that I came from
It can get lonely when you're travelling hard
But you can even be lonely standing in your own backyard

Nobody knows the existential dread
Of the things that go on inside someone else's head
Whether it be trivial or something that Dante said
But, baby, nobody knows the meaning of loneliness

No matter how well you know someone you can only ever guess
How can you ever really know somebody else?
It takes more than a lifetime just to get to know yourself
Nobody knows the meaning of loneliness

I have to say a word about solitude
For the soul it, sometimes they say, can be good
And I'm partial to it myself, well, I must confess
Nobody knows the meaning of loneliness

Well, there's Sartre and Camus, Nietzsche and Hesse
If you dig deep enough you gonna end up in distress
And no one escapes having to live life under duress
And no one escapes the meaning of loneliness

Well, they say keep it simple when it gets to be a mess
And fame and fortune never brought anyone happiness
I must be lucky, some of my friends think that I'm really blessed
Nobody knows the meaning of loneliness

No, no, no, no, no, no, nobody knows the meaning of loneliness
No, no, no, no, nobody knows the meaning of loneliness
Nobody knows the meaning of loneliness

Stranded

I'm stranded at the edge of the world
It's a world I don't know
Got nowhere to go
Feels like I'm stranded

And I'm stranded between that ol' devil and the deep blue sea
Ain't nobody's gonna tell me
Tell me what, what time it is

Every day, every day, it's hustle, hustle time, hustle time
Every day and every way, one more, one more mountain to
  climb

It's leaving me stranded in my own little island
With my eyes open wide
But I'm feeling stranded

Every, every, every day, it's hustle time
Every way, one more mountain to climb

I'm stranded between the devil and the deep blue sea
There ain't nowhere else to be
'Cept right here and I'm stranded

Pay the Devil

One man's meat is another man's poison
One man's gain can be another man's loss
I'm travelling down the lonely highway
'Cause a rolling stone don't gather no moss

Once I thought I could live the kind of life I wanted
But the wayward wind made me restless and a fool of me
'Cause I thought I could settle for the nine-to-five life
Well, I guess it just was never meant to be

Now people talk and they speculate about what other people
  would do
But they can't put themselves within my shoes
It used to be my life, now it's become my story
I'm heading down this highway with those blues

Well, I'd love to see the sun setting on the riverside
Just to go back home and I want to settle down
Well, I have to pay the devil for my music
Why I have to keep on with this roaming around?

Have to pay the devil for my music
Keep on rolling from town to town
Have to pay the devil for to play my music
Keep on rolling from town to town

This Has Got to Stop

I've given you my heart and my soul
I've given you more than you'll ever know
I've given you just about everything I can
Can't you see that I'm just only one man?

I took you out to the picture show
Then I took you walkin' outdoors
I walked you up and down the block
Then I warned you, 'Baby, this has got to stop'

This has got to stop, you're way over the top
Pack my things and walk, we can't even talk
This has got to stop, I just had enough
I'm gonna call your bluff, walk you one more lap

And I watched you watching me as I watched you walk away
from me
And I went off to that far country
I took a plane out to that Newfoundland
When you said to me that you didn't understand

This has got to stop, you're way over the top
I'm gonna pack my things and walk, we don't even talk
This has got to stop, baby, I just had enough
I'm gonna call your bluff, walk me one more lap

Well, I came back home and I burnt our house down
I watched it crumble to the ground
Oh it caved in like a piece of balsa wood
I turned to you and said, 'Baby, this is just no good'

And I worked and I tried to build it all back up again
The day you told me that you had really changed
Then you knocked down all my castles in the sand
Then I said, 'Baby, I know now just where we stand'

This has got to stop, you're way over the top
Pack my bags and walk, we don't even talk
This has got to stop, I've just had enough
I'm gonna call your bluff, this has got to stop

This has got to stop
Stop, stop, I've had enough
I'm gonna call your bluff
Stop, stop, stop
This has got to stop

End of the Land

When too many demands have destroyed all my plans
Going down to the end of the land
If I have to drive all night just to feel alright
Going down to the end of the land

When it gets out of hand and I fail to agree
Just what's in it for me?
Going down to the sea

Then I've got to run towards the setting sun
Going down to the end of the land

When it gets out of hand and I beg to disagree
Just what's in it for me?
Get back down to the sea

And then I've got to run to the setting sun
Going down to the end of the land
If I've got to drive all night till the morning light
I'm going down to the end of the land

Going down, going down, going down to the end of the land
Going down to the end of the land

Song of Home

Well, it's written in the wind
For the story does begin
I will go back to my kin across the sea
There's a bird that's on the wing and it's flying free
He can hear the song of home endlessly

Well, the further I must go
Then the nearer I must stay
Men have sailed the seven seas to be free
And like that bird that's on the wing and is flying free
He can hear the song of home endlessly

I can see the harbour lights
Hear the foghorns in the night
All up and down the lough, calling

From the rocky shores of Maine
I will sail back home again
Back to where my heart longs to be
And the bird that's on the wing and is flying free
He can hear the song of home endlessly

I can see the harbour lights
Hear the foghorns in the night
Boats up and down the lough, calling, calling

From the rocky shores of Spain
I will sail back home again
Back to where my heart will always be
Just like a bird that's on the wing and is flying free
He can hear the song of home endlessly

He can hear the song of home endlessly
He can hear the song of home endlessly

Soul

Soul is a feeling, feeling deep within
Soul is not the colour of your skin
Soul is the essence, essence from within
It is where everything begins

Soul is what you've been through
What's true for you
Where you going to
What you're gonna do

Soul is your station or the folk of your nation
Something that you wear with pride
Soul can be your vision or something that is hidden
It's not something that you gotta hide

Soul is what you've been through
And what's true for you
Where you going to
What you're gonna do

Soul can be your station or the folk of your nation
Something that you wear with pride
Soul can be your vision, it can be your religion
Something that you just can't hide

Soul is a feeling, feeling deep within
Soul is not the colour of your skin
Soul is the essence, essence from within
Soul is where everything begins

Mystic of the East

Mystic of the East, mystic from the streets
Mystic with no brief, back here on the street
Mystic out of reach, can't find no reason to speak
I just got in too deep for the mystic of the East

I was deep in the heart of Down
Deep in the heart of Down
Deep in the heart of Down
Deep in the heart

Mystic with no peace, back here in the East
Fed up to the teeth, mystic of the East

I was deep in the heart of Down
Deep in the heart of Down
Deep in the heart of Down
Deep in the heart

Mystic out of reach, can't seem to find my brief
Gone with the wild geese and I've had it up to the teeth
Mystic of the East, back here on the streets
Mystic with no brief, I can't find any reason to speak

Mystic of the East, East, East, East
Back here on the street, back on the street
Back on the street, mystic of the East
Back here on the street, mystic of the East

KEEP 'ER LIT

Introduction *by Eamonn Hughes*

Van Morrison's status as an original is assured. In his early work with Them he led one of the great bands to emerge from the British blues boom, kickstarted the pop and rock scene in Ireland, and also wrote songs that have not just endured but entered the canon of popular music. Striking out on his own he then changed the way that music sounded by ignoring the lines along which it had been developing in favour of his own unique combination of sounds and words. Since then he has continued to move restlessly across forms and genres, rarely feeling any need to conform to prevailing fashions or values in either his words or his musics (and the plural is appropriate). Anyone looking for patterns in his work will quickly recognise that the overarching pattern is of disruption. As soon as he has established a sound or a set of concerns, he moves on to something different. In doing so he has produced songs that are simply necessary in the lives of the many people who use them to mark the significant moments – both joyful and melancholy – in their lives.

This is the second volume of Van Morrison's selected lyrics and it aims, like its predecessor, *Lit Up Inside* (2014), to provide a representative sample of his work. Just flicking through the book and noticing the different shapes of the songs gives an immediate sense of the many different ways that Morrison has approached the art of songwriting from tightly controlled early lyrics through more free-flowing songs or even spoken word pieces into what look like more conventional song structures. Taken together the two volumes give an overview of his work over some fifty years as a songwriter. The arrangement here is once again broadly chronological and the songs again cover a range of themes, topics, places, and people that manages to be both extensive and concentrated. Van Morrison has both extended the range of, for want of a better term, the popular song and equally he has established and returned to a core set of concerns and interests throughout his career.

Even a partial list of his recurrent interests is still extensive. It would have to include love songs, work songs (about both physical work and the work of being a songwriter), songs about the pains and anxieties of existence, songs of consolation, songs about various kinds of spiritual quest and the realms of the mystical, and songs which deal with healing and reconciliation both with the self and with others. Then there are the songs of memory and of childhood; songs about the natural world ('nature's bright green shady path' as it's called in 'Rave On, John Donne') and about the perspectives it can provide on time, which can exist both in various secular forms (the seasons, times of day) and *sub specie aeternitatis*. Places too receive due attention both in the naming of many actual towns and cities and in the form of semi-mythical locations. There are songs of falling leaves and evening shadows, of joyous sounds and whining boy moans; there are songs of wisdom and grace. There is also a long-standing concern with the 'the voice of the silence' ('Little Village'), and many tributes to the voices of musicians and writers who have been significant for Morrison.

This brief listing points in two directions. On the one hand it is possible to break these categories down into specifics. The love songs, for example, deal with love in all its guises: the just glimpsed, the domestically settled, the anguish of break-ups, the ways in which an earthy, secular love can slide almost imperceptibly into something more spiritual, the idea that love can provide an afternoon of joy, or a lifetime of meaning. Likewise, it's possible to find songs for every season of the year, and indeed for most times of the day. Contrariwise these various categories slide into and across each other: gardens as places in the natural world are also echoes of the primal mystical garden and are the setting for many love songs whether rapturous or melancholy, while the love being expressed can be either profane or spiritual (and sometimes both). There is here a basic opposition. On the one hand there is the desire of the observer and recorder of experience to note as clearly as possible the details of that experience, as in, for example, 'It was on a Sunday and the autumn leaves were on the ground' ('If You and I Could Be As Two'). For this songwriter the time of day, the weather, the season of the year, the location are all vital aspects of the experience – the emotion being recollected (whether tranquilly or not) is inextricably tied up with such details and the songs are faithful to them. This can be true even when the songs are elliptical, fragmented and episodic. Songs such as 'Astral Weeks' seem to arise from a sense of being overwhelmed and as a result all the recorder can do is out pick out occasional details from a welter of stimuli – 'pictures on the walls / Whispering in the halls . . . clean clothes . . . little red shoes' – catching them on the fly as tokens of the many impressions that the receptive consciousness of the speaker / writer is open to. Song after song confronts the world in this way: as a result when reading through the songs we can't help but notice the many things that are recorded: cigarettes, fishing rods, radios, train tracks, shoes, combs, coats, accordions to list just a few of the inanimate kind, a list that can be doubled and redoubled if we move into the natural, the animate, and the human world. As against this impulse there is the contrary one which seeks to bring everything into something like harmony, to abstract from the welter of sense impressions some overarching vision in which a song can be about all things simultaneously. These impulses can be seen as centrifugal and centripetal, forces pulling in opposite directions, and taking our lead from this we can see how Morrison's body of work is marked by a number of similarly oppositional forces. There are the songs that forbid looking back, and the songs steeped in memory; there are the songs that assert the need to dwell in the particular moment and the songs that search for the transcendent; the songs of joy in this world and the songs warning against the material world (including those in which the music business is excoriated). Again this list of oppositions could be continued to encompass the whole body of work. The obvious immediate response to this point is to quote from Walt Whitman (named in 'Rave On, John Donne Part II'): 'Do I contradict myself? / Very well then I contradict myself, / (I am large, I contain multitudes.)' That would certainly be one way of thinking about Morrison's songs as a body of work, but to leave it there would also be a disservice to that work by implying that there is an irresolution at the heart of it. It is better, then, to consider these various oppositions as foundational contradictions in line with (to take another of Morrison's references) William Blake's 'Without Contraries is no progression.' From very early on the situation of lovers in Morrison's songs echoes this sense of opposition: 'And there go you and I / Between the earth and sky' ('My Lonely Sad Eyes'). In doing so it also slides between sacred and secular forms of love. Of course, in saying this we are pointing not just to Blake (and a number of other writers besides Blake) but also to the traditions of soul, blues and gospel music in which this elision of the sacred and profane is central.

Which brings us to the question of where Van Morrison stands in relation to tradition and how that relates to his undoubted originality. In 'Goldfish Bowl' he refers to 'Jazz, Blues & Funk . . . Folk with a beat / And a little bit of Soul' which is a good starting point (though by no means the destination) for thinking about his relationship to tradition. We tend to see the artist, at least since the period of the Romantics, as a singular, even solitary, figure, forging ahead with their work while ignoring all others. Equally, at least since Ezra Pound insisted in the early twentieth century that his fellow writers should 'make it new', a premium has been placed on the notion of the original and the modern. Both T. S. Eliot and W. B. Yeats argued against Pound and for tradition – as Yeats put it 'even what I alter must seem traditional . . . Ancient salt is best packing.' But both also had some difficulties in defining tradition and how the artist relates to it. Academic writing on this subject has tended to stress what is called the 'anxiety of influence': the idea that any artist, to borrow a phrase from James Joyce, 'frets in the shadow' of his or her predecessors.

Van Morrison can be classified, in the available terms, as a 'solo artist', he is a singer, a songwriter, and a musician, but we know that this classification is only part of the story. Van Morrison is also a bandleader, a frequent collaborator with other singers in his live shows (and on *Duets* he works with sixteen other singers), and a singer and musician who has covered a range of others' songs. That last point is worth dwelling on. Surveying Morrison's recorded work it's hard to overlook his practice of covering of songs by other writers which started with Them and has continued throughout his career. This may seem like a strange point with which to introduce a book of Van Morrison's lyrics, but it offers a way into those lyrics.

Without wishing to turn this introduction into an exercise in allusion spotting (others have done a more comprehensive job than would be possible here) it is worth noting that Morrison's songwriting and his covers of others' work are interdependent. For example, when he covers Sister Rosetta Tharpe's 'How Far from God' on *Roll with the Punches* in 2017 it fits comfortably with the songs that he has written on just this subject. At one level this explains why singers pick songs to cover: the chosen song allows them a variant on a familiar form of expression. But there is something else happening here. What also makes the song familiar within the context of Morrison's work is its repeated phrase 'walk and talk' which appears early in Morrison's writing ('If You and I Could Be As Two', 'Sweet Thing') and the activity, if not the actual words, appear in many other songs ('If I Ever Needed Someone', 'Autumn Song'). It's a common enough phrase and it would be foolish to say that it is an allusion to the Tharpe song, but it fits into a larger pattern. Morrison's own songs are steeped in tropes and themes acquired over a lifetime of listening and performing: in 'Foggy Mountain Top' he notes that he has 'been listening to this music / Ever since the age of three'. It seems to be as natural as breathing for him, then, to begin a song such as 'Give Me My Rapture' with two lines – 'There are strange things happening every day / I hear music up above my head' – which can be confidently identified as allusions to a Sister Rosetta Tharpe song and to a gospel song made famous by her. Given that this is a spiritual song it is not surprising to find a reference to the idea of the 'dark night of the soul' from St John of the Cross later in the lyric. All of these references might well be considered traditional regardless of their source. By making use of them Morrison is then placing himself within a form of music (and within other forms of writing as well) and might be seen as adapting the tradition to make his own plea for spiritual enlightenment. There is a twist to this, however, in that another version of 'Strange Things Happening', by Etta James, is about an altogether more profane and earthy form of rapture, the very temptation that Morrison's song wishes to resist. 'Give Me My Rapture', then, we could say, is traditional but, more importantly, it is so only because it is part of a tradition that Morrison is creating and mobilising within his work. His songs are, then, a way of walking and talking with tradition.

This is just one example of how Morrison's songs relate to the several traditions from which they derive. Tharpe is an easier, because more limited, example to deal with than some others; the engagements with William Blake or John Lee Hooker, with W. B. Yeats or Hank Williams are much more expansive. It should go without saying, but it is worth stressing, that these engagements are not all one way. These four names would not fit together in any other context than Morrison's work. Morrison, in other words, is not drawing on some existing tradition; rather he is creating, adding to, and modifying his own tradition as he writes. In contrast to some other ideas of tradition and how artists relate to it, Morrison's engagement is confident and generous; it is hard to think of another writer who is so open to naming and sharing sources, models, inspirations. If the radio brought much of this work to his attention, then it's as if his songs have now become an equivalent to the radio from which others can learn. There is little sense here of any anxiety or fretfulness. Instead, there is a joyous cataloguing of predecessors who are celebrated and honoured, treated with generosity and given their due by someone who stands confidently in line with them as an equal, someone who has created his own tradition by creating his own body of work. Steeped though they are in traditions, we never have any doubt that we are hearing a Van Morrison song. Where else would you find William Wordsworth, Lawrence Ferlinghetti and Jon Hendricks being brought together in a way that makes sense? Van Morrison's songs are, then, a conversation both with himself and with this ever-developing tradition. When he rhymes 'crossroads' with 'arcadian groves' in 'Pagan Heart' he brings both Robert Johnson and W. B. Yeats into the conversation, and we are reminded that although they are near contemporaries, there is nowhere else but in Morrison's work that such a connection would be made. We can therefore look to his work not just for what it does in its own right but also for how it can reshape our sense of cultural connections.

Paradoxically, it is this kind of engagement with the tradition that he has created that is one of the most original aspects of Van Morrison's writing. Without him this tradition would not exist. When you get to the final words of this book ('The Prophet Speaks') what you are reading is another part of Van Morrison's life-long conversation with the tradition that he has shaped, not just for himself but for us as well: 'Come closer now / I'll tell you with a whisper'.

If You and I Could Be As Two

It was on a Sunday and the autumn leaves were on the
ground
Kicked my heart when I saw you standing there in your dress
of blue
The storm was over, my ship sailed through
What is this feeling, what can I do?

If you and I could be relieved to walk and talk
And be deceived I'd give my all and all
And more I would do
If darling only you and I could be as two

If we could dream and by our dreams
Sew this wicked world up at the seams
I'd give my life, and more I would do
If darling only you and I could be as two

Baby do you remember
All the good times we had together
Walkin' through the park
Baby then, then we could sing
Give you all my money
Everything in the world that I have
You told me that don't mean a thing

If still in darkness
We could run together there
In that morning sun
I'd give my all, my love and everything to you
If darling only you and I could be as two
Could be as two

Could be as two
Could be as two

Bad or Good

Everybody's got some soul
I don't care if they're young or old
Gotta hold on, when all is gone
Make out like it's fine

While we say yeah (bad or good)
Oh Yeah (bad or good)
Yeah, yeah, yeah, yeah, yeah, yeah (bad or good)
Gotta let it happen (bad or good)
Everybody (bad or good)
Sometime, oh yeah

Don't even have to say one word
It ain't nothin that we've seen or heard
Get out, get out, jump back child
Make like you know what it's all about

And we say yeah (bad or good)
Oh Yeah (bad or good)
Oh baby (bad or good)
Gotta let it happen (bad or good)
Everybody (bad or good)
Sometime, some sweet time

If there's something, baby, you want me to do
Come on over here and I'll see about you
Yeah I'll make it, shake it all about
Jump back child

Just say yeah (bad or good)
Oh Yeah (bad or good)

Oh Yeah (bad or good)
Gotta let it happen (bad or good)
Everybody (bad or good)
Sometime, sometime, oh yeah

Could You Would You

Could you, would you, hold me in your arms
Show me all your charms or make me sad or make me blue
Could you love me, like I love you, like I love you?

Could you, would you, squeeze and hold me tight
Love me all through the night, never ever let me go
Could you love me, like I love you so, like I love you so?

Every time I see you walkin' down my avenue
I say hi hi hi hi hi, are you alright?
You say how do you do
Just like you always do
But if I had you in my arms tonight

Could you, would you, hold me oh so near
While I whisper in your ear
The sweet words, you long to hear
Could you love me, like I love you, like I love you?

Could you, would you, hold me oh so near
While I whisper in your ear
The sweet words, you long to hear
Could you love me, like I love you, like I love you,
Just like I love you?

Friday's Child

From the North to the South
You walked all the way
You know you left your home
Left your home for good to stay

While you built all
All your castles in the sun
And I watched you knock 'em down
Knock 'em down, each and every one

Oh, Friday's child, you can't stop now, no
Oh, Friday's child, you can't stop now

And I watched you before you came too old
And I told you, a long time before
You ever came to be told
You got somethin' that they all wanna know
You gotta hold on and never, never let go

Oh, Friday's child, you can't stop now, no, no
Oh, Friday's child, you cannot stop now
You can't stop

There you go,
There you go with rainbows hangin' round your feet
And you're makin' out
You're makin' out with everyone that you meet
You're even having a ball and staying out late
And watched the sun come up round Notting Hill Gate

Oh, Friday's child, you can't stop now, no, no

Oh, Friday's child, you cannot stop, you're driving
No, no, no, no, no, no, no, no, no, no
You cannot stop now,
It's too much
You can't stop
You can't stop
You can't stop

One Two Brown Eyes

Went out last night walkin'
I heard someone talkin'
You'd better stop stayin' out late at night
Straighten up and fight
Right you better stop tellin' those lies
Gonna cut you down to my size
You got one, you got two brown eyes
Hypnotize, hypnotize, hypnotize
Yeah, Yeah, oh
Oh, oh, oh, oh,
Oh, oh, oh, oh

You got such pretty good looks
You don't really find in good books
You'd better stop staying out late at night
Or straighten up and fight, right
I gonna cut you down to my size
You got one, two brown eyes
Hypnotize
Oh what eyes
Hypnotize
Yeah, yeah, oh
Oh, oh, oh, oh,
Oh, oh, oh, oh

You Just Can't Win

One more coffee, one more cigarette
One more morning trying to forget
If I had a chance to join your dance
I wouldn't like to bet your game is something

Yet it's a shame
Ain't natural for you
Baby it's a sin
You know you just can't win
When you are in

You used to ride on buses
Take a tube to Camden Town
Now you go by aeroplane
Don't let nothing bring you down

Yet it's a shame
Ain't natural for you
Baby it's a sin
You know you just can't win
When you are in

Now the road is dark and lonely
But you got to bear the load
You're up in Park Lane now
I'm somewhere round the Tottenham Court Road

Yet it's a shame
Ain't natural for you
Baby it's a sin
You know you just can't win

When you are in

No, you just can't win
No, you just can't win
When you are in

The Smile You Smile

The smile you smile is you
And I see through your laughing eyes
The smile you smile is you
And I see through your laughing eyes, oh baby
And in the whirlpool of them
I can be in paradise

And I'd go roamin' in the gloamin'
Ever and a day with you,
I'd go roamin' in the gloamin'
Ever and a day with you
And sit between the stars and say
That that's my point of view

I-I-I-I-I love you
I-I-I-I-I love you

And talk to trees and sunshine
Feel your lips against my lip
And talk to trees and sunshine
Feel your lips against my lip
And smell your sweet perfume
And even touch your fingertips

I-I-I-I-I love you
I-I-I-I-I love you
I-I-I-I-I love you

Astral Weeks

If I ventured in the slipstream
Between the viaducts of your dreams
Where immobile steel rims crack
And the ditch in the back roads stop

Could you find me
Would you kiss my eyes
And lay me down in the silence easy
To be born again, to be born again?

Far from the side of the ocean
If I put the wheels in motion
And I stand with my arms behind me
And I pushed another door

Could you find me
Would you kiss my eyes
Lay me down in the silence easy
To be born again, to be born again?

There you go standing with the look of Avarice
Talking to Huddie Ledbetter
Showing pictures on the walls
Whispering in the halls
And pointing a finger at me

There you go, there you go
Standing in the sun darling
With your arms behind you
And your eyes before

There you go
Taking care of your boy
Seeing that he's got clean clothes
Putting on his little red shoes
Seeing that he's got clean clothes
Putting on his little red shoes
Pointing a finger at me

And here I am
Standing in your sad arrest
Trying to do my very best
Looking straight at you
And coming through, darling

If I ventured in the slipstream
Between the viaducts of your dreams
Where immobile steel rims crack
And the ditch in the back roads stop

Could you find me
Would you kiss my eyes
And lay me down in the silence easy
To be born again, to be born again?

To be born again, to be born again

In another world, darling
In another world
In another time
Got a home on high

Ain't nothing but a stranger in this world
I'm nothing but a stranger in this world
I got a home on high
In another land so far away, so far away

Way up in the heaven
Way up in the heaven
Way up in the heaven
Way up in the heaven

In another time
In another place
In another time
In another place
Way up in the heaven
In another time
In another place
In another time
In another place
And another face

Sweet Thing

And I shall stroll the merry way and jump the hedges first
And I will drink clear clean water for to quench my thirst
And I shall watch the ferry boats and they'll get high
On a blue ocean against tomorrow's sky

And I will never grow so old again
And I will walk and talk in gardens all wet with rain
Oh, oh, oh sweet thing
Sweet thing, sweet thing
Oh, my, my, my sweet thing

I shall drive my chariot down your streets and cry
'Well it's me and I'm dynamite and I don't know why'
And you shall take me strongly in your arms again
And I wonder if I might remember that I ever felt the pain

We shall walk and talk in gardens all misty wet
All misty wet with rain down on
And I will never, never, never grow so old again
Oh, oh sweet thing
Oh, oh, oh you sweet thing
Sweet thing
My, my, my,

And I will raise my hands up into the nighttime sky
And count the stars that's shining in your eye
And just to dig it all not to wonder that's just right
And I'll be satisfied not to read in between the lines

And I will walk and talk in gardens all wet with rain
And I will never ever, ever, ever grow so old again

Oh, oh sweet thing
Oh, oh, oh, sugar baby
Oh, oh, sweet thing
Sugar baby
Sugar baby
Sugar baby
What a champagne eye
And your sweet light smile

And It Stoned Me

Half a mile from the county fair
And the rain came pourin' down
Me and Billy standin' there
With a silver half a crown
Hands are full of fishin' rod
And the tackle on our backs
We just stood there gettin' wet
With our backs against the fence

Oh, the water
Oh, the water
Oh, the water
Hope it don't rain all day

And it stoned me to my soul
Stoned me just like Jelly Roll
And it stoned me
And it stoned me to my soul
Stoned me just like goin' home
And it stoned me

And the rain let up and the sun came up
And we were getting' dry
Almost let a pick-up truck nearly pass us by
So we jumped right in and the driver grinned
And he dropped us up the road
And we looked at the swim and we jumped right in
Not to mention fishing poles

Oh, the water
Oh, the water

Oh, the water
Let it run all over me

And it stoned me to my soul
Stoned me just like Jelly Roll
And it stoned me
And it stoned me to my soul
Stoned me just like goin' home
And it stoned me

On the way back home we sang a song
But our throats were getting dry
Then we saw the man from across the road
With the sunshine in his eye
Well he lived all alone in his own little home
With a great big gallon jar
There were bottles too, one for me and you
And he said, 'Hey, there you are.'

Oh, the water
Oh, the water
Oh, the water
Get it myself from the mountain stream

And it stoned me to my soul
Stoned me just like Jelly Roll
And it stoned me
And it stoned me to my soul
Stoned me just like goin' home
And it stoned me
And it stoned me to my soul
Stoned me just like Jelly Roll
And it stoned me
And it stoned me to my soul
Stoned me just like goin' home
And it stoned me

Crazy Love

I can hear her heart beat from a thousand miles
And the heavens open every time she smiles
And when I come to her that's where I belong
Yet I'm running to her like a river song

She give me love, love, love, love, crazy love
She give me love, love, love, love, crazy love

She got a fine sense of humour when I'm feeling low down
And when I come to her when the sun goes down
Take away my trouble, take away my grief
Take away my heartache, in the night like a thief

She give me love, love, love, love, crazy love
She give me love, love, love, love, crazy love

Yeah I need her in the daytime
Yeah I need her in the night
Yeah I want to throw my arms around her
And kiss her hug her kiss and hug her tight

And when I'm returning from so far away
She give me some sweet lovin' brighten up my day
And it make me righteous, and it make me whole
And it make me mellow down to my soul

She give me love, love, love, love, crazy love
She give me love, love, love, love, crazy love
She give me love, love, love, love, crazy love
She give me love, love, love, love, crazy love

Caravan

And the caravan is on its way
I can hear the merry gypsy play
Mama, mama look at Ammaro
She's a-playing with the radio
La, la, la, la, la, la, la
La, la, la, la, la, la, la

And the caravan has all my friends
It will stay with me until the end
Gypsy Robin, Sweet Ammaro
Tell me everything I need to know
La, la, la, la, la, la, la
La, la, la, la, la, la, la

Turn up your radio and let me hear the song
Switch on your electric light
Then we can get down to what is really wrong
I long to hold you tight so I can feel you
Sweet lady of the night I shall reveal you

If you will
Turn it up, turn it up, little bit higher, radio
Turn it up, burn it up, so you know, radio
La, la, la, la, la, la, la
La, la, la, la, la, la, la

And the caravan is painted red and white
That means everybody's staying overnight
And the barefoot gypsy boy round the campfire sing and play
And a woman tells us of her way

La, la, la, la, la, la, la
La, la, la, la, la, la, la

Turn up the radio and let me hear the song
Switch on your electric light
Then we can get down to what is really wrong
I long just to hold you tight so baby I can feel you
Sweet lady of the night I shall reveal you

If you will
Turn it up, turn it up, little bit higher, radio
Turn it up, that's enough, so you know it's got soul
Radio, radio, turn it up,
La, la, la, la, la, la, la, la, la, la, la, la, la, la

Come Running

By the side of the tracks where the train goes by
The wind and the rain will catch you, you will sigh
Deep in your heart
Then you'll come running to me
You'll come running to me

Well you watch the train go round the bend
Play in dust and dream that it will never end
Deep in your heart
You'll come running to me
You'll come running to me

Said, hey, come running to me
Oh, come running to me
Hey, yeah, come running to me
Said, hey, come running to me
Oh, come running to me
Hey, yeah, come running to me

With your hound dog by your side
And your arms stretched out open wide
I wanna keep you satisfied in the morning sun
By my side, come on, come on run

Well alright hey, in the country
Kick the sand up with your heels
You think to yourself how good it feels
Put away all your walking shoes
Then you come running to me
Hey, yeah, now you come running to me

I said, hey, come running to me
Oh, come running to me
Hey, yeah, come running to me
Hey, come running to me
Oh, come running to me
Hey, yeah, come running to me
Come on, come on, run
Come on run
Come on run
Come on run
Come running
Come on
Run to me

You gotta rainbow if you run to me

These Dreams of You

I dreamed you paid your dues in Canada
And left me to come through
I headed for there right way
I knew exactly just what to do
I dreamed we played cards in the dark
And you lost and you lied
Wasn't very hard to do
But hurt me deep down inside

These dreams of you
So real and so true
These dreams of you
So real and so true

My back was up against the wall
And you slowly just walked away
You never really heard my call
When I cried out that way
With my face against the sun
You pointed out for me to go
Then you said I was the one
Had to reap what you did sow

These dreams of you
So real and so true
These dreams of you
So real and so true

And hush-a-bye, don't ever think about it
Go to sleep and don't ever say one word
Close your eyes, you are an angel sent here from above

And Ray Charles was shot down
But he got up to do his best
A crowd of people gathered round
To the question answered, 'yes'
And you slapped me on the face
I turned around the other cheek
You couldn't really stand the pace
And I would never be so meek

These dreams of you
So real and so true
These dreams of you
So real and so true

And hush-a-bye, hush-a-bye don't ever think about it
Go to sleep, don't ever say one word
Close your eyes, you are an angel sent here from above
And hush-a-bye, hush-a-bye don't ever think about it
Go to sleep, don't ever say one word
Close your eyes

Everyone

We shall walk again, all along the lane
Down the avenue just like we used to
With our heads held high smile at passers by
Then we'll softly sigh ay, yi, yi, yi, yi, yi

Everyone, everyone, everyone, everyone
Everyone, everyone, everyone, everyone

By the winding stream we shall lay and dream
And make dreams come true if we want them to
And so overcome play the pipes and drum
Sing a happy song and we'll sing along

Everyone, everyone, everyone, everyone
Everyone, everyone, everyone, everyone

We shall walk again all along down the lane
Down the avenue just like we used to
With our heads held high smile at passers by
Then we'll softly sigh ay, yi, yi, yi, yi, yi

Everyone, everyone, everyone, everyone
Everyone, everyone, everyone, everyone

Domino

Don't want to discuss it
I think it's time for a change
You may get disgusted
Start thinking that I'm strange
In that case I'll go underground
Get some heavy rest
Never have to worry
About what is worst and what is best

I said, Oh, Oh Domino
Roll me over, Romeo
Lord have mercy, I said
Oh, Oh Domino
Roll me over, Romeo, there you go
Say it again, I said
Oh, Oh Domino
I said Oh, Oh Domino

There's no need for argument
There's no argument at all
And if you never hear from him
That just means he didn't call
Or vice versa
That depends on wherever you're at
And if you never hear from me
That just means I would rather not

Oh, Oh Domino
Roll me over, Romeo
There you go
Lord have mercy, I said

Oh, Oh Domino
Roll me over Romeo
There you go
Say it again
Oh, Oh Domino
I said Oh, Oh Domino

Hey Mr DJ
I just want to hear some rhythm and blues music
On the radio
On the radio
On the radio

Virgo Clowns

Let us free you from the pain
Let us see you smile again
Let us unlock all the chains
You're broken hearted

Let us help you to forget
Let us help you unlock it
It's not nearly time to quit
You've only started

You gotta
Sit down funny face
Let your laughter fill the room
Light up your golden smile
Take away all your misery and gloom
Let your laughter fill the room
Let your laughter fill the room

Let us shake you by the hand
Let us help you understand
Take your head out of the sand
And shake it free now

Let us help you to go on
We are here to lean upon
Now you know exactly just who
You want to be now

Sit down funny face
Let your laughter, let your laughter fill the room
Light up your golden smile

Take away all your misery and gloom
Let your laughter fill the room
Let your laughter fill the room

Let us lift you up on high
See the twinkle in your eye
Raise you up into the sky
And say it's easy

Hey let the trumpets ring it
Let the angels sing it
Let your pretty feet go dancing
Let your worn out mind go prancing
Sit down funny face
Let your laughter fill the room
Light up your golden smile
Take away all your misery and gloom
Let your laughter fill the room
Let your laughter fill the room
Let your laughter fill the room
Let your laughter fill the room
Let it fill the room
Let it fill the room
Let your laughter fill the room

If I Ever Needed Someone

Lord if I ever needed someone I need you
Lord if I ever needed someone I need you

To see me through the daytime
And through the long lonely night
To lead me through the darkness
And on into the light
To stand with me when I'm troubled
And help me through my strife
When times get so uncertain to turn to you
Turn to you in my young life

Lord if I ever needed someone I need you
Lord if I ever needed someone I need you

Someone to hold on to
And keep me from all fear
Someone to be my guiding light
And keep me ever dear
To keep me from my selfishness
To keep me from my sorrow
To lead me on to givingness
So I can see a new tomorrow

Lord if I ever needed someone I need you
Lord if I ever needed someone I need you

Someone to walk with
Someone to hold by the hand
Someone to talk with
Someone to understand

To call on when I need you
And I need you very much
To open up my arms to you
And feel your tender touch
To feel it and to keep it
Just right here in my soul
And care for it and keep it with me
Never to grow old

Lord if I ever needed someone I need you
Lord if I ever needed someone I need you
Lord if I ever needed someone I need you
Lord if I ever needed someone I need you

Wild Night

As you brush your shoes
And stand before the mirror
And you comb your hair
Grab your coat and hat
And you walk wet streets
Tryin' to remember
All the wild night breezes
In your memory ever.

And everything looks so complete
When you're walkin' out on the street
And the wind catches your feet
And sends you flyin', cryin'
Oooh-wee
The wild night is calling
Oooh-wee
The wild night is calling

And all the girls walk by
Dressed up for each other
And the boys do the boogie-woogie
On the corner of the street
And the people passin' by
Just stare in wild wonder
And the inside juke-box
Roars out just like thunder.

And everything looks so complete
When you walk out on the street
And the wind catches your feet
And sends you flyin', cryin'

Oooh-wee
The wild night is calling
Oooh-wee
The wild night is calling

The wild night is calling
The wild night is calling
Come on out and dance
Come on out and make romance
Come on out and dance
Come on out and make romance

The wild night is calling
The wild night is calling
Come on out and dance
Come on out and make romance
Come on out and dance
Come on out and make romance

I Wanna Roo You (Scottish Derivative)

Twenty third of December, covered in snow
You in the kitchen with the lights way down low
I'm in the parlour playing my old guitar
Speaking to you, darling, find out how you are
I wanna roo you, wanna get through to you
I wanna woo you, woo you tonight
I wanna roo you, wanna get through to you
I wanna woo you, woo you tonight

Come to me softly, come to me quiet
Know what I'm after and I'm gonna try it
Snowstorm's on the way and we'll be stranded for a week
Come over to the window, look outside take a peek
I wanna roo you, wanna get through to you
I wanna woo you, woo you tonight
I wanna roo you, wanna get through to you
I wanna woo you, woo you tonight

You know I am lonely and in need of your company
Oh, let your love light shine on down on me

And we can just sit here, look at the fire
Watch the flames leaping higher and higher
Tea on the stove, food in the pan
Ain't going nowhere and we don't have many plans
I wanna roo you, wanna get through to you
I wanna woo you, woo you tonight
I wanna roo you, wanna get through to you
I wanna woo you, woo you tonight

And you know I am lonely

I been in need of your company
Let your love, let your love this morning
Shine on down on me
I wanna roo you, wanna get through to you
I wanna woo you, woo you tonight
I wanna roo you, wanna get through to you
I wanna woo you, woo you tonight
Woo you tonight, pretty baby
Woo you tonight, little darling
Woo you tonight, it's alright
Woo you tonight

I Will Be There

Whenever the sunshine comes through
Whenever my thoughts turn to you
Whatever you want me to do
I will be there

Whether I crawled up the hill
Child you know I've been through the mill
Just as long as I fit the bill
I will be there

If it's on a lazy afternoon in summertime
And you're drinkin' champagne and wine
Any time I don't mind
And even if I've got the blues
After I've paid all my dues
And you decide to go for a cruise
I will be there

And If it's on a lazy afternoon in summertime
And you're drinkin' champagne and wine
Any time I don't mind
And even if I've got the blues
On account of paying oh so many dues
And you decide to go for a cruise

Gonna grab my razor and my suitcase
And my toothbrush, and my overcoat
And my underwear
I will be there

Redwood Tree

Boy and his dog
Went out looking for the rainbow
And oh, what did they learn
Since that very day

Walking by the river
And running like a blue streak
Through the fields and streams and meadows
Laughing all the way

Oh Redwood Tree
Please let us under
When we were young we used to go
Under the Redwood Tree

And it smells like rain
Maybe even thunder
Won't you keep us from all harm
Wonderful Redwood Tree

And a boy and his father
Went out, went out looking for the lost dog
And oh what, oh what have they learned
Since they did that together

They did not bring him back
He already had departed
But look at everything they have learned
Since that, since that very day

Oh Redwood Tree

Please let us under
When we were young we used to go
Under the Redwood Tree

And it smells like rain
Maybe even thunder
Won't you keep us from all harm
Wonderful Redwood Tree

Autumn Song

Leaves of brown they fall to the ground
And it's here, over there leaves abound
Shut the door dim the lights and relax
What is more, your desire, or the facts

Pitter patter the rain falling down
Little glimmer sun coming round
Take a walk when autumn comes to town

Little stroll past the house on the hill
Some more coal on the fire if you will
And in a week or two it'll be Halloween
Set the page and the stage for the scene

Little game the children will play
And as we watch them while time away
Look at me and take my breath away

You'll be smiling eyes beguiling
And the song on the breeze
Will call my name out
In your dreams

Chestnuts roasting outside as you walk
With your love by your side
The old accordion man plays mellow
and bright
And you go home in the crispness of
the night

Little later friends will be along

And if you feel like joining the throng
Just might feel like singing autumn song
Just may feel like

You'll be smiling
Eyes beguiling
And the song on the breeze
Calls my name out in your dreams

Chestnuts roasting outside
As you walk with your love by your side
And the old accordion man plays mellow, mellow and bright
And you go home in the crispness of the night

Little later friends will be along
And if you feel like joining the throng
Just might feel like singing autumn song
Just may feel like singing autumn song

You just may break out
You just may break out
You just may
You just may have to break out
You just may
You just may have to lose control
You just may have to lose control
'Cause you got it in your soul
You just may
Just may have to break out
You just may
You just may have to break out

Break out
Hear what I'm singing
Way out in the distance

Way out in the distance
Way over in the corner
Way out in the distance
Cable car
And I hear the church bells chime
And I hear the church bells chime
Way out in the distance
Way out in the distance
Infinitesimal
Beauty of your eyes
Catches me in my starlight
Gazing, gazing
And I'm embracing something
Turn around
Hand on my shoulder
Saying
It's so peaceful
It's so peaceful
Inside
Inside
Inside
I believe I've
I believe I've
Transcended myself child
Transcended myself child
Transcended myself child

Mechanical Bliss

Mechanical bliss is striking me for what I believe in
The ribbon on the line, and getting in and getting out
Was not like this

No, mechanical bliss was not like this at all

The ribbon on the line, and getting in and getting out
Was not like this, was not like this, was not like this

Caruthers and Smith said that they couldn't come at all

They said that their backs were up against the wall

And getting in and getting out
Was not like this, was not like this, was not like this

But a flash of the list, the flick of a switch

A flick of a switch, you gave me a kiss, I couldn't resist
No, mechanical bliss

Now Ponsonby-Smith said he really didn't care

About Neville and Chippy who really wasn't there

And getting in and getting out
Was not like this, was not like this

He's out in the sun, he's sucking his thumb

He's talking to Hun

Oh, mechanical bliss

Mechanical bliss was not like this
Mechanical bliss was not like this at all

The ribbon on the line and getting in and getting out
Was not like this, was never, never like this

I couldn't resist the flash of the list, a flick of the switch
The lisp, you talked in a lisp, you gave me a kiss

You talked in a lisp, you talked in a lisp
Mechanical bliss

O.K. Chaps, stiff upper lip!

Fair Play

Fair play to you
Killarney's lakes are so blue
And the architecture I'm taking in with my mind
Is so fine

Tell me of Poe
Oscar Wilde and Thoreau
Let your midnight and your daytime
Turn into love of life

It's a very fine line
But you've got the mind child
To carry it on when it's just about to be carried on

And there's only one meadows way to go
And you say Geronimo
And there's only one meadows way to go
And you say Geronimo

A paperback book as we walk down the street
Fill my mind with tales of mystery, mystery
And imagination
Forever fair
And I'm touching your hair
I wish we would be dreamers in this dream
Oh, oh let it be

And there's only one meadows way to go
And you say Geronimo
And there's only one meadows way to go
And you say Geronimo

Fair play to you
Killarney's lakes are so blue
Hi ho silver tit for tat
And I love you for that

Hi ho silver tit for tat
And I love you for that
Love you for that
Love you for that
Hi ho silver tit for tat
Tit for tat
And I love you for that
Hi ho silver tit for tat
And I love you for that

And there's only one meadows way to go
And I say Geronimo
And there's only one meadows way to go
And we say Geronimo, Geronimo

And there's only one meadows way to go
And we say Geronimo
And there's only one meadows way to go
And we say Geronimo

Fair play to you

Linden Arden Stole the Highlights

Linden Arden stole the highlights
With one hand tied behind his back
Loved the moon and sun and whiskey
Ran like water in his veins

Loved to go to church on Sunday
Even though he was a drinkin' man
When the boys came to San Francisco
They were lookin' for his life

But he found out where they were drinkin'
Met them face to face outside
Cleaved their heads off with a hatchet
Lord he was a drinkin' man

And when somebody tried to get above him
He just took the law into his own hands
Linden Arden stole the highlights
And he put his fingers through the glass

He had heard all the stories many, many times before
And he did not care no more to ask
And he loved the little children
Like they were his very own

He said say some day it may get lonely
Now he's living, living with a gun

Who Was That Masked Man?

Oh ain't it lonely when you're living with a gun
Well you can't slow down and you can't turn around
And you can't trust anyone

You just sit there like a butterfly
And you're all encased in glass
You're so fragile you just may break
And ya don't know who to ask

Oh ain't it lonely when you're living with a gun
Well you can't slow down and you can't turn around
And you can't trust anyone

You just sit there like a butterfly
You're well protected by the glass
You're such a rare collector's item
When they throw away what's trash

You can hang suspended from a star
Wish on a toilet roll
You can just soak up the atmosphere
Like a fish inside a bowl

When the ghost comes round at midnight
Well you both can have some fun
He can drive you mad, he can make you sad
He can keep you from the sun

When they take him down he'll both be safe and sound
And the hand does fit the glove
And no matter what they tell you
There's good and evil in everyone

Streets of Arklow

And as we walked
Through the streets of Arklow
Oh the colour
Of the day wore on
And our heads
Were filled with poetry
In the morning
A-comin' on to dawn

And as we walked
Through the streets of Arklow
In gay profusion
In God's green land
And the gypsies rode
With their hearts on fire
They say 'We love to wander,
Lord we love,
Lord we love to roam.'

And as we walked
Through the streets of Arklow
In all its raging beauty
Rolling back to the day
And I saw your eyes
They was shining, sparkling crystal clear
And our souls were clean
As the grass did grow
And our souls were clean
As the grass did grow
And our souls were clean
As the grass did grow

And as we walked
Through the streets of Arklow

You Don't Pull No Punches but You Don't Push the River

When you were a child, you were a tomboy
Gimme soul satisfaction
Way back in shady lane
Do you remember darlin'

And it's the woman in you, and it's the woman in you
Gimme soul satisfaction
And it takes the child in you to know
The woman an' you are one

We're goin' out in the country to get down to the real soul,
I mean the real soul, people,
We're talkin about real soul people
We're goin' out in the country, get down to the real soul
We're gettin' in to the west coast
Shining our light into the days of bloomin' wonder
Goin' as much with the river as not, as not,
An' I'm goin' as much with the river as not

Blake and the Eternals, standin' with the Sisters of Mercy
Looking for the Veedon Fleece,
William Blake and the Eternals, standin' with the Sisters of Mercy
Looking for the Veedon Fleece.

You don't pull no punches, but you don't push the river
You don't pull no punches, and you don't push the river
You don't pull no punches, and you don't push the river, no, no
Goin' as much with the river as not

We're goin' out in the West, down to the cathedrals
We're goin' out in the West, down to the beaches
And the Sisters of Mercy, behind the sun
Oh behind the sun

And William Blake and the Sisters of Mercy looking for the Veedon Fleece,
You don't pull no punches, goin' West, goin' as much with the river as not
With the river as not, with the river as not, goin' as much,
Goin' as much with the river as not, no,
You don't pull no punches, and you don't push the river, no
You don't pull no punches, but you don't push the river, no
You don't pull no punches, but you don't push the river, no
You don't pull no punches, but you don't push the river

And we was contemplating Baba, William Blake and the Eternals
Goin' down to the Sisters of Mercy
Looking for the Veedon Fleece
Looking for the Veedon Fleece
Looking for the Veedon Fleece

You don't pull no punches, but ya, you don't push the river
You don't pull no punches, but ya, you don't push the river, no
You don't pull no punches, but ya, you don't push the river
You don't push the river, you don't push the river

You Gotta Make It through the World

Well let them take you for a clown
And they're bound to bring you down
You got to make it through the world if you can
Think they're doing you wrong
But you got here on your own
You got to make it through the world if you can
I said if you can, if you can
You got to make it through the world if you can
I said if you can, if you can
You got to make it through the world if you can

Well you know without a doubt
Nobody know you when you're down and out
You got to make it through the world if you can
Well talk about wrong and right
You've got to make up your own mind
You got to make it through the world if you can

I said if you can, if you can
You got to make it through the world if you can
I said if you can, well if you can
You got to make it through the world if you can

Yeah, let them take you for a clown
They will surely put you down
You got to make it through the world if you can
Everybody talk about wrong and right
You got to make up your own mind about it
You got to make it through the world if you can

Oh, if you can, if you can
You got to make it through the world if you can

Yeah, if you can, if you can
You got to make it through the world if you can
Yeah I said if you can, Lord, if you can
You got to make it through the world if you can

I said you got to make through the world if you can
I said you got to make through the world if you can
I said you got to make through the world if you can
You got to make it through the world if you can

Make it through the world
Make it through the world
Make it through the world
Make it through the world
Make it through the world
Got to make it through the world

The Eternal Kansas City

Excuse me do you know the way to Kansas City?
Excuse me do you know the way to Kansas City?
Excuse me do you know the way to Kansas City?
Excuse me do you know the way to Kansas City?

Train down to St Louis in Missouri
Over to the city there, you know that one
Where the farmer's daughter digs the farmer's son
Dig your Charlie Parker
Basie and Young
Witherspoon and Jay McShann
It will come

Excuse me do you know the way to Kansas City?
Excuse me do you know the way to Kansas City?
Excuse me do you know the way to Kansas City?
Excuse me do you know the way to Kansas City?

Lady Liberty is waiting
You know she lights the way
Her name is Billie, she's a Holiday
And the city is eternal, can't you see?
It's inside of you and it's inside of me

You know, you know the way to Kansas City
You know, you know the way to Kansas City
You know, you know the way to Kansas City
You know, you know the way to Kansas City
You know, the way to Kansas City
You know, the way to Kansas City
Wham-Bam

(You know the way to Kansas City)
Thank you Ma'am
(You know the way to Kansas City)
Sing it
You know the way to Kansas City
Hey
You know the way to Kansas City
You know the way to Kansas City
You know the way to Kansas City
You know the way to Kansas City
You know
The way to Kansas City one time

(You know the way to Kansas City)
(You know the way to Kansas City)
(You know the way to Kansas City)
(You know the way to Kansas City)
(You know the way to Kansas City)

Joyous Sound

How sweet that joyous sound
Whenever we meet, whenever we meet
How sweet that joyous sound
Whenever we meet again

I think you'll know it well
Whenever we meet, whenever we meet
I think you'll know it well
Whenever we meet again

Just let it in and let it out
And you will begin to know without a doubt

That grace will follow us
Wherever we go, wherever we go
That grace will follow us
Until we meet again

Just let it in and let it out
And you will begin to know without a doubt

That grace will follow us
Wherever we go, wherever we go
That grace will follow us
Until we meet again

How sweet that joyous sound
Whenever we meet, whenever we meet
How sweet that joyous sound
Whenever we meet again
Whenever we meet

Whenever we meet
Whenever we meet again
Whenever we meet
Whenever we meet
Whenever we meet again
Whenever we meet
Whenever we meet
Whenever we meet again

Flamingos Fly

Go for a ride
In the still of the night
And morning brings forth
All its wonderful delight
Couldn't have made it more plain
When I heard that soft refrain
And I heard you gently sigh

Wanna take you where flamingos fly, flamingos fly
Way over yonder in the clear blue sky
That's where flamingos fly

Lie in the dark
With the sound of the nightingale
Listen for a lark
I will tell you a tale
Breeze is blowin', blowin' outside
Wanna take that moonlight ride
When I heard you gently sigh

Wanna take you where flamingos fly, flamingos fly
Way over yonder in the clear blue sky
That's where flamingos fly

Well we're here and we're waiting
For that morning light to shine
And I'm looking at you, looking at me, looking right back at
  you
And I'm anticipating signs along the way
Looking at you, looking at me, looking right back at you

I'll follow the road
That will take me, take me right back home
And carry that load
Where the deer and the provincial angels roam
Happiness touches, touches me now
I know where it came from and how
When I heard you gently sigh

Wanna take you where flamingos fly, flamingos fly
Way over yonder in the clear blue sky
That's where flamingos fly, flamingos fly
Way over the rooftops of the houses
I heard it one time, I heard it one time in a lullaby
I heard it one time, I heard it one time in a lullaby
Somewhere, somewhere, somewhere
Way over the rooftops of the houses
Heard it one time in a lullaby
Heard it one time, heard it one time in a lullaby

Checkin' It Out

We've got to put our heads together
I'm sure that we can work it out
I'm weighin' up the situation
And checkin' it out
Takin' it further
Takin' it further
Checkin' it out

This is a workin' situation
I'm tellin' you without a doubt
We've gotta pull it all in tight, baby
Checkin' it out
Takin' it further
Takin' it further
Checkin' it out

And all the obstacles along the way
Sometimes may feel so tremendous
There are guides and spirits all along the way
Who will befriend us

Let's talk it out across the table
Make sure that we leave nothin' out
Get in to it like a meditation
Start checkin' it out
Takin' it further
Takin' it further
Checkin' it out

And all the obstacles along the way
Sometimes may feel so tremendous

There are guides and spirits all along the way
Who will befriend us

Let's talk it out across the table
Make sure that we leave nothin' out
Get in to it like a meditation
Start checkin' it out
Takin' it further
Takin' it further
Checkin' it out

Checkin' it out, now baby
Checkin' it out, checkin' it out
You meditate, you meditate
You meditate
And you come back, you come back
You bring it up now baby
You bring it up now baby
You bring it up
You bring it up now
In your loving cup

Natalia

I'm walkin' down the street
I'm on that midnight beat
I'm on a lonely avenue
Baby, won't you walk with me
Baby, won't you talk with me
Oh, that's all I want you to do, now
Walk with me
Talk to me
Call your name out

Na Na, Na Na, Na Na
Na Na, Na Na, Na Na
Na Na, Na Na, Na Na Natalia

Here on a summer night
I wanna kiss and hold you tight
Just the way we used to do
Walkin' down the same old street
People that we used to meet
Such a long, long time ago, now
Walk with me
Talk to me
And I call out your name

Na Na, Na Na, Na Na
Na Na, Na Na, Na Na
Na Na, Na Na, Na Na Natalia
Na Na, Na Na, Na Na
Na Na, Na Na, Na Na
Na Na, Na Na, Na Na Natalia
On a magic night like this

I hunger for your kiss
On a magic night like this

Na Na, Na Na, Na Na
Na Na, Na Na, Na Na
Na Na, Na Na, Na Na Natalia
Na Na, Na Na, Na Na
Na Na, Na Na, Na Na
Na Na, Na Na, Na Na Natalia

Walk with me
Talk with me
Walk with me
Talk with me
Walk with me
Talk with me
Walk with me
Talk with me
Walk with me baby
Talk with me

Natalia, Natalia, Natalia
Natalia, Natalia, Natalia

Lifetimes

You sit in silence
And the river answers
And I have loved you many, many years
I saw you standing by the wondrous river
And I have come today
To calm your fears

Those lifetimes
So many lifetimes
With you

The boatman singin' far across the water
What is this feelin' in my heart and soul
The nighttime angel spreads her wings
Around me
And I feel the sadness
And the river flows

Those lifetimes
So many lifetimes
With you

Listen to the music inside
That is all that you have to do
Listen to the music inside
Can't you hear what it says to you

And I shall get to know you
In these lifetimes
In awe and wonder
On down through the years

The nighttime angel spreads her wings
Around me
I feel the silence
And my doubts are cleared

Those lifetimes
So many lifetimes
With you

Listen to the music inside
That is all that you have to do now
Listen to the music inside
Can't you hear what it says to you

Listen to the music inside
That is all that you have to do now
Listen to the music inside
Can't you hear what it says to you

Listen to the music inside
Can't you hear
Can't you hear what it says to you
Can't you hear what it says to you now
You gotta sit right down
Sit right down and listen to the music inside
That is all, that is all, that is all, that is all
That you have to do now
Listen, listen, listen
To the music, the music
The music, the music
That is all that you have to do

Hungry for Your Love

I'm hungry for your love
I'm hungry for your love
I'm hungry for your love
But I can wait now

I'm on the telephone
And I am all alone
I'm on the telephone
And we're connected

I got such a lot of love
I wanna give it to you
I got such a lot of love
I wanna give it to you
I got such a lot of love
I wanna give it to you

And though we're far apart
You are here in my heart
And though we're far apart
You're part of me now

And after all the years
And after all the tears
And after all the tears
There's just the truth now

I got such a lot of love
I wanna give it to you
I got such a lot of love
I wanna give it to you

I got such a lot of love
I wanna give it to you

Well, I'm hungry for your love
Hungry for your love
Well, I'm hungry, yeah, well, I'm hungry
For your love now

I love you in buckskin, yeah, yeah
I love you in buckskin, yeah, yeah
I love you, I love you, I love you, I love you
I love you, I love you, I love you, I love you
I love you, I love you, I love you

I'm hungry for your love

Take It Where You Find It

Men saw the stars at the edge of the sea
They thought great thoughts about liberty
Poets wrote down words that did fit
Writers wrote books
Thinkers thought about it

Take it where you find it
Can't leave it alone
You will find a purpose
To carry it on
Mainly when you find it
Your heart will be strong
About it

Many's the road I have walked upon
Many's the hour between dusk and dawn
Many's the time
Many's the mile
I see it all now
Through the eyes of a child

Take it where you find it
Can't leave it alone
You will find a purpose
To carry it on
Mainly when you find it
Your heart will be strong
About it

Lost dreams and found dreams
In America

In America
In America
Lost dreams and found dreams
In America
In America
In America

And close your eyes
Leave it all for a while
Leave the world
And your worries behind
You will build on whatever is real
And wake up each day
To the new waking dream

Take it where you find it
Can't leave it alone
You will find a purpose
To carry it on
Mainly when you find it
Your heart will be strong
About it

Lost dreams and found dreams
In America
In America
In America
Lost dreams and found dreams
In America
In America
In America

Change come over
Talkin' about a change
Change come over

Change come over
Change come over
Change, change, change
Change, change, change
Change, change, change
I'm talkin' about a
Change, change, change
Change, change, change
Change come over
Sing it to me now

I'm gonna walk down the street
Until I see
My shining light
I'm gonna walk down the street
Until I see
My shining light
I'm gonna walk down the street
Until I see
My shining light
I'm gonna walk down the street
Until I see
My shining light
Here it comes
I see my light
See my light
See my shining light
I see my light
See my light
I see my shining light
I see my light
See my light
See my shining light
I see my light
See my light

See my shining light

Lost dreams and found dreams
In America
In America
In America
Lost dreams and found dreams
In America
In America
In America
Lost dreams and found dreams
In America
In America
In America
Lost dreams and found dreams
In America
In America
In America

Full Force Gale

Like a full force gale
I was lifted up again
I was lifted up again by the Lord

No matter where I roam
I will find my way back home
I will always return to the Lord

In the gentle evening breeze
By the whispering shady trees
I will find my sanctuary in the Lord

I was heading for a fall
And I saw the writing on the wall

Like a full force gale
I was lifted up again
I was lifted up again by the Lord

I was heading for a fall
And I looked up and saw the writing on the wall

In the gentle evening breeze
By the whispering shady trees
I will find my sanctuary in the Lord

No matter where I roam
I will find my way back home
I will always return to the Lord

Like a full force gale

I was lifted up again
I was lifted up again by the Lord

I was lifted up again
Lifted up
I said I was lifted up, by the Lord
Lifted up again, lifted up again
Lifted up again, by the Lord

You Make Me Feel So Free

Some people spend their time
Just running round in circles
Always chasing some exotic bird
I prefer to spend some time
Just listening for that special something
That I never ever had
I'd like a new song to sing
Another show or somewhere entirely different to be
But, baby you make me feel so free

And so I yearn for mistress calling me
That's the muse, that's the muse
But we only burn up with the passion
When there's absolutely nothing
Left to lose
I'll make it to spring
And there's no bed of roses
It's just more hard work in bad company
But, baby I want to say this, you make me feel so free

I heard them say that
You can have your cake and eat it
But all I wanted was just one free lunch
How can I eat it when the man that's next to me now
He grabbed it Lord he beat me
Beat me to the punch
How can I even talk about freedom when you know
Oh it's a sweet mystery but baby, you, you
You make me feel so free

I'm gonna lay my cards here

Right down on the table
And spin a wheel and roll the dice
And whatever way it comes out
And whatever way it turns out
Baby, you know, well that's the price
Well I'll order again there's no need to explain
I just need somewhere to dump all my negativity
But baby remember, you make me feel so free

What you say, what you say, what you say
What you say, what you say
What you say, what you say, what you say, what you say
What you say, what you say, what you say, what you say
You make me feel so free baby
Say it, say it, say it again
You make me feel so free
So doggone free

Steppin' Out Queen

Put on your lipstick
Apply your make-up
Sometimes you'll be livin'
Livin' in a dream
And then and then
Then you go stepping out queen

Then you go to a party
And you laugh loud and hearty
And you stay all night long
Oh you know you make the scene
And then you go stepping out queen

Do do do do, do do do do, do do 'n do
Stepping out
Do do do do, do do do do, do do 'n do

It's just a windfall
Just a windfall away
It keeps getting stronger every day
Baby you got to look out and say
It's a windfall away

Do do do do, do do do do, do do 'n do
Do do do do, do do do do, do do 'n do

It's just a windfall away
It's a love, it's a love, it's a love
Keeps getting stronger every day
You got to look up and say
It's a windfall away

Do do do do, do do do do, do do ’n do
It’s just a windfall away
Do do do do, do do do do, do do ’n do

Well you go through the drama
And you work in the dharma
And you stand up
Stand up and wipe
Wipe your mirror clean
As you go stepping out queen

Do do do do, do do do do, do do ’n do
Stepping out
Do do do do, do do do do, do do ’n do

(Come in the garden and just look at the flowers)
This is the windfall way
(We can just sit and talk for hours and hours)
It’s a love, keeps getting stronger, every day
(Come in the garden and just look at the flowers)
This is the windfall way
(We can just sit and talk for hours and hours)
It’s a love, it’s a love, it’s a love, it’s a love, it’s a love,
(Come in the garden and just look at the flowers)
Come in the garden and then we’ll go
(We can just sit and talk for hours and hours)
Stepping out, stepping out, stepping out

Troubadours

From the ancient sun to the old hearth stove
Sing the troubadours
From the city gates to the castle walls
Come the troubadours

On a sunlit day it was bright and clear
And the people came from far and they came from near
To hear the troubadours
Do do do do do do do do, do do do do

And the troubadours sang their songs of love
To the lady fair
She was sitting outside on her balcony
In the clear night air

It was a starry night and the moon was shining bright
And the trumpets rang and they gave a chime
For the troubadours
Do do do do do do do do, do do do do

And for every man all across the land
And from shore to shore
They come singing songs of love and chivalry
From the days of yore

Baby lift your window high do you hear that sound
It's the troubadours
As they go through town
With their freedom song, do do do do

Oh baby lift your window high do you hear that sound

It's the troubadours
With their freedom vow,
do do do, do do do do do, do, do, do, do

Baby, baby, baby lift your window high turn your lamp down low
Don't you know I love you so
Do you hear that sound; do you dig that sound
It's the troubadours coming through town

Satisfied

Let's go walkin' up that mountainside
Look down in the valley down below
And we survey this wondrous scene
Wait a minute
Hold that dream
Hold that dream

I want to change my name and write a book
Just like *Catcher in the Rye*
Settle down in a shady nook
Talkin' to my baby now

I'm satisfied
With my world
'Cause I made it
The way it is
Satisfied, satisfied,
Satisfied, satisfied,
Satisfied, satisfied,
Inside

Go to the mountain
Come back to the city
There's a whole lot of things
Don't look very pretty
Spiritual hunger and spiritual thirst
But you got to change it
On the inside first
To be satisfied
To be satisfied

Sometimes I think I know where it's at
Other times I'm completely in the dark
You know, baby, cause and effect
I got my karma from here right to New York

I'm satisfied
With my world
'Cause I made it
The way it is
Satisfied, satisfied
Satisfied, satisfied
Satisfied, satisfied
Inside

Sometimes I think I know how it is
Other times I'm completely in the dark
You know, baby, cause and effect
And I got my karma from here right to New York
I'm satisfied
'Cause I made it
The way it is
I'm satisfied, satisfied
Satisfied, satisfied
Satisfied, satisfied
Inside

I'm satisfied, satisfied

Wild Honey

Open your arms in the early mornin'
When the light comes shinin' through
Can't you hear my heart beat just for you
It's beating so wild, honey
And light comes shinin'

Singin' my song
And the band is playin'
And the music is tried and true
Can't you hear my heart beat just for you
It's beating so wild, honey
And light comes shinin'

I'll be waiting for you
I'll be waiting here for thee
Way up on the mountain
Where the hillside rolls down to the sea

Tell me what's real
What I feel inside
Any time of day or night will do
It's alright
Can't you hear my heart beat just for you
It's beating so wild, honey
And your light comes shining through

Tell me what's real
What I feel inside
Any time of day or night will do
It's alright
Can't you hear my heart beat just for you
It's beating so wild, honey

And the light comes shining through
And the light comes shining through
It's beating so wild, so wild, so wild, so wild, so wild, so
And the light comes shining through
And the light comes shining
And the light comes shining through

When Heart Is Open

And when heart is open
And when heart is open
You will change just like a flower slowly openin'
And when heart is open
You will change just like a flower slowly openin'
When there's no comin'
And there's no goin'

And when heart is open
You will meet your lover
You will tarry
You will tarry
In an old country

And when heart is open
You will meet your lover
When there's no comin'
And there's no goin'

Oh, hand me down my greatcoat
Oh, hand me down my greatcoat
I believe I'll go walkin' in the woods
Oh, my darlin'
Oh, hand me down my big boots
Oh, hand me down my big boots
I believe I'll go walkin' in the woods
Oh my darlin'

And she moves by the waterfall
When she moves
She moves just like a deer
Across the meadow

And when heart is open
You will change just like a flower slowly openin'
When there's no comin'
And there's no goin'
You will tarry
With your lover
And when heart is open you will meet your lover

Oh, hand me down my greatcoat
Oh, hand me down my greatcoat
I believe I'll go walkin' in the woods
Oh, my darlin
Oh, hand me down my big boots
Oh, hand me down my big boots
I believe I'll go walkin' in the woods
Oh, my darling
Oh, when she moves
She moves like a deer across the meadow

When heart is open
You will change just like a flower slowly openin'
You will change just like a flower slowly openin'

You will change just like a flower slowly openin'
When there's no comin'
When there's no comin'
And there's no goin'
You will meet
You will meet your lover
When there's no comin'
And there's no goin'
You will meet
You will meet your lover

Haunts of Ancient Peace

In haunts of ancient peace
We walk in haunts of ancient peace
At night we go to sleep and rest
In haunts of ancient peace

The love and light we seek
The words we do not need to speak
In haunts of ancient peace

We seek the Holy Grail
In haunts of ancient peace
The vision of the New Jerusalem*
Be still in haunts of ancient peace

We seek the Holy Grail
In haunts of ancient peace
And build the New Jerusalem
In haunts of ancient peace

Be still in haunts of ancient peace
Be still in haunts of ancient peace
In haunts of ancient peace
In haunts of ancient peace

* William Blake indicated the New Jerusalem was Glastonbury.

Northern Muse (Solid Ground)

And she moves on the solid ground
And she shines light all around
And she moves on the solid ground
In the County Down

And she moves on the solid earth
And she knows what her wisdom is worth
And she moves on the solid ground
In the County Down

She lifts me up, fill my cup
When I'm tired and weary, Lord
And she keeps the flame
And she give me hope
To carry on

If you see her, say hello
For she's someone that I surely know
When I was young
She made me roam from my home
In the County Down

And she moves on the solid ground
And she moves in the County Down
In the County Down

Inarticulate Speech of the Heart

Inarticulate speech, inarticulate speech of the heart
Inarticulate speech, inarticulate speech of the heart
Inarticulate speech, inarticulate speech of the heart
Inarticulate speech, inarticulate speech of the heart

I'm a soul in wonder, I'm a soul in wonder
I'm a soul in wonder, I'm a soul in wonder

Inarticulate speech, inarticulate speech of the heart
Inarticulate speech, inarticulate speech of the heart

I'm just wild about it, I can't live without it
I'm just wild about it, I can't live without it

Inarticulate speech, inarticulate speech of the heart
Inarticulate speech, inarticulate speech of the heart

I'm a soul in wonder, I'm a soul in wonder
I'm a soul in wonder, I'm a soul in wonder

I'm a soul in wonder, a soul in wonder
I'm a soul in wonder, I'm a soul in wonder
I'm a soul in wonder

A soul in wonder, I'm a soul in wonder
A soul in wonder, I'm a soul in wonder

A Sense of Wonder

I walked in my greatcoat down through the days of leaves
No before after, yes after before
We were shining our light into the days of blooming wonder
In the eternal presence, in the presence of the flame

Didn't I come to bring you a sense of wonder?
Didn't I come to lift your fiery vision bright?
Didn't I come to bring you a sense of wonder in the flame?

On and on and on we kept singing our song
Through Newtownards and Comber, Gransha and the
  Ballystockart Road
With Spike and Boffyflow, I said I would describe the leaves
  for Samuel and Felicity
Rich, red, browny, half burnt orange and green

Didn't I come to bring you a sense of wonder?
Didn't I come to lift your fiery vision bright?
Didn't I come to bring you a sense of wonder in the flame?

It's easy to describe the leaves in autumn
And it's oh so easy in the spring
But down through January and February
It's a very different thing

On and on and on, through the winter of our discontent
When the wind blows up the collar and the ears are
  frostbitten too
I said I could describe the leaves for Samuel and what it
  means to you and me
You may call my love Sophia, but I call my love Philosophy

Didn't I come to bring you a sense of wonder?
Didn't I come to lift your fiery vision bright?
Didn't I come to bring you a sense of wonder in the flame?

Didn't I, didn't I come to bring you a sense of wonder?
Didn't I come to lift your fiery vision bright?
Didn't I come to bring you a sense of wonder in the flame?

In the flame child
A sense of wonder in the flame
In the flame child

Wee Alfie at the
Castle Picture house on the Castlereagh Road
Whistling on the corner next door where
He kept Johnny Mack Brown's horse
'O Solo Mio' by McGimsey
And the man who played the saw
Outside the City Hall
Pastie suppers down at Davy's Chipper,
Gravy rings, Wagon Wheels
Barmbracks, Snowballs

A sense of wonder
A sense of wonder
A sense of wonder

On and on and on
And on and on and on

And after the days of leaves
And after the days of leaves

Oh the Warm Feeling

Oh the warm feeling
As we sat beside the sea
Oh the warm feeling
As I sat by you

Like a child within the kingdom
As we sat beside the sea
Oh the warm feeling
As I sat by you

And it filled me with devotion
And it made me plainly see
And it healed all my emotions
As I sat by you

As we sat inside the sunshine
As we sat beside the sea
Oh the warm feeling
As I sat by you

And it filled me with religion
And it gave great comfort to me
Oh the warm feeling
As I sat by you

Oh the warm feeling
As we sat beside the sea
Oh the warm feeling
As I sat by you

A Town Called Paradise

Copycats ripped off my songs
Copycats ripped off my words
Copycats ripped off my melody
It doesn't matter what they say
It doesn't matter what they do
All that matters is
My relationship to you

Gonna take you out
Get you in my car
We're goin' go for a long, long, long drive
We're goin' down
To a town called Paradise
Down where we can be free
We're gonna drink that wine
We're gonna jump for joy
In a town called Paradise

We're going up the mountainside
Child you can look for miles
And see the vision in the West
We're gonna swing round and look north
To south, east and west
And go round in a circle too

And we're gonna start dancing
Like we've never danced before
I'm gonna take you in my arms
I'm gonna squeeze you tight
Say everything will be alright
We're gonna get that squealing feeling

Gonna take you down
Baby to a town called Paradise
Down where we can be free
It doesn't matter what they say
It doesn't matter what they do
All that matters is my relationship to you
We're gonna ride all night long
All along the ancient highway
Gonna be there when the morning comes

By the river we will linger
As we drive down, down to be free
Paradise when we're dancing
Paradise in my Imagination too
Paradise with my Willpower
Paradise

Queen of the Slipstream

You're the queen of the slipstream
With eyes that shine
You have crossed many waters to here
You have drank of the fountain of innocence
And experienced the long, cold wintry years

There's a dream where the contents are visible
Where the poetic champions compose
Will you breathe not a word of this secrecy
And will you still be my special rose?

Going away far across the sea
But I'll be back for you
I will tell you everything I know
Tell me everything that's true

Will the blush still remain on your cheeks my love?
Is the light always seen in your head?
Gold and silver they placed at your feet my dear
But I know you chose me instead

Going away far across the sea
But I'll be back for you
I will tell you everything I know
Tell me everything that's true

You're the queen of the slipstream
I love you so
You have crossed many waters to be here
And you drank at the fountain of innocence
An experience you know very well

You're the queen
Queen of the slipstream
The queen of the slipstream
See you slipping and sliding in the snow
Queen of the slipstream
You come running to me
You come running to me
Queen of the slipstream

Give Me My Rapture

There are strange things happening every day
I hear music up above my head
Fill me up with your wonder
Give me my rapture today

Let me contemplate the presence so divine
Let me sing all day and never get tired
Fill me up from your loving cup
Give me my rapture today

Won't you guide me through the dark night of the soul
That I may better understand your way?
Let me be just worthy to receive
All the blessings from the Lord into my life

Give me my rapture today
Give me my rapture today
Love fill me up
From your loving cup
Give me my rapture today

Let me purify my thoughts and words and deeds
That I may be a vehicle for thee
Let me hold to the truth I know in the darkest hour
Let me sing in the glory of the Lord

Give me my rapture today
Give me my rapture today
Give me my rapture today

Contacting My Angel

Contacting my angel, contacting my angel
She's the one, she's the one that satisfies
Contacting my angel she's the one that satisfies
She's the one that I adore

Got a telepathic message from my baby
In a little village through the fog
Here comes my baby, I can tell, I can tell
By the way she walks
Said I've been on a journey up the mountainside
And I drank the water from the stream
It was pure
Pure water and it healed me

I met a presence on the mountainside
And he looked so radiant and he was the
Youth of eternal summers
Like a sweet bird of youth in my soul
In my soul, in my soul, in my soul
In my soul, in my soul, in my soul

I'd Love to Write Another Song

I'd love to write another song
But nothing seems to come
I'd love to write another song
To carry me along
Make some money, pay the bills
Keep me busy too
I'd love to write another love song

I'd love to write another song
I'm searching everywhere
Though I look for inspiration
Sometimes it's just not there
I have to work, I have to play
I have to get in step
If I could write another love song
I know it sure would help

I'd love to write another song
Baby especially for you
I'd love to write another song
And feel things bright and new
In poetry I'd carve it well
I'd even make it rhyme
I'd love to write another song
Just to get some peace of mind

I'd love to write another song
To get some peace of mind

I'd love to write another song
Baby for some peace of mind

I'm Tired Joey Boy

I'm tired Joey boy
While you're out with the sheep
My life is so troubled
That I can't go to sleep
I would walk myself out
But the streets are so dark
I shall wait till the morning
And walk in the park

This life is so simple
When one is at home
And I'm never complaining
When there's work to be done
Oh I'm tired Joey boy of the makings of men
I would like to be cheerful again

Ambition will take you and ride you too far and
Conservatism bring you to boredom once more

Sit down by the river
And watch the stream flow
Recall all the dreams
That you once used to know
The things you've forgotten
That took you away
To pastures not greener but meaner

Love of the simple is all that I need
I've no time for schism or lovers of greed
Go up to the mountain, go up to the glen
When silence will touch you
And heartbreak will mend

Daring Night

In the daring night
When all the stars are shining bright
Squeeze me don't leave me
In the daring night
Galactic swirl in the firmament tonight
Oh with the lord of the dance
With the lord of the dance
In the daring night

I see Orion and the Hunters
Standing by the light of the moon
In the daring night
In the daring night

And the heart and the soul
As we look up in awe and wonder at the heavens
Oh and we go with the lord of the dance
With the lord of the dance
With the lord of the dance
In the daring night

In the daring night
When all the stars are shining bright
Oh baby squeeze me don't leave me
In the daring night

In the firmament we move
We move, we move and we live
And we have our being
Squeeze me don't leave, leave me
In the daring night

In the firmament we move and galactic swirl
And we live and we breathe and we have our being
Baby in the daring night
Darling squeeze me, squeeze me
Don't ever leave me
In the daring night
When all the stars are shining bright

And don't let go, and don't let go
Don't let go, don't let go
In the daring night
And we move and we move, and we move and we move
And we move and we move and we move
Baby don't let go
In the daring night

In the daring night
When all the stars are shining bright
Baby squeeze me don't leave me
In the daring night

Capture it all
With the lord of the dance
Oh with the lord of the dance
In the daring night
With the lord of the dance
With the lord of the dance
And the great goddess of the eternal wisdom
Standing by the light of the moon
In the daring night

And the bodies move
And we sweat and have our being
Baby don't leave me
In the daring night

In the daring night
When all the stars are shining bright
Squeeze me don't leave me
Baby in the daring night
Baby in the daring night
In the daring night

Squeeze me don't leave me
In the daring night
In the daring night
In the daring night
And don't let go
Don't let go
Don't let go

Real Real Gone

Real, real gone
I got hit by a bow and arrow
Got me down to the very marrow
And I'm real, real gone

Real, real gone
I can't stand up by myself
Don't you know I need your help?
And I'm real, real gone

Some people say you can make it on your own
Oh you can make it if you try
I know better now you can't stand up alone
Oh baby that is why

I'm real, real gone
I can't stand up by myself
Don't you know I need your help?
You're a friend of mine
And I'm real, real gone

And Sam Cooke is on the radio
And the night is filled with space
And your fingertips touch my face
You're a friend of mine
And I'm real, real gone

I'm real gone
Oh lord I got hit by a bow and arrow
Got me down to the very marrow
You're a friend of mine

And I'm real, real gone
And I'm real, real gone
I'm real gone

Wilson Pickett said:
'In the midnight hour, that's
When my love comes tumbling down'

Solomon Burke said:
'If you need me, why don't you call me?'

James Brown said:
'When you're tired of what you got, try me'

Gene Chandler said:
'There's a rainbow in my soul'

Enlightenment

Chop that wood
Carry water
What's the sound of one hand clapping?
Enlightenment, don't know what it is

Every second, every minute
It keeps changing to something different

Enlightenment, don't know what it is
Enlightenment, don't know what it is
It says it's non-attachment, non-attachment, non-attachment

I'm in the here and now, and I'm meditating
And still I'm suffering but that's my problem
Enlightenment, don't know what it is

Wake up

Enlightenment says the world is nothing
Nothing but a dream
Everything's an illusion and nothing is real

Good or bad baby
You can change it any way you want
You can rearrange it
Enlightenment, don't know what it is

Chop that wood
And carry water
What's the sound of one hand clapping?
Enlightenment, don't know what it is

All around baby, you can see
You're making your own reality, every day because
Enlightenment, don't know what it is

One more time

Enlightenment, don't know what it is
It's up to you
Enlightenment, don't know what it is
It's up to you every day
Enlightenment, don't know what it is
It's always up to you
Enlightenment, don't know what it is
It's up to you, the way you think

Youth of 1000 Summers

He's the youth of a thousand summers
He's the youth of a thousand summers
Like a sweet bird of youth
Like a sweet bird of youth
In my soul, in my soul, in my soul
In my soul, in my soul, in my soul

And he looks so radiant
And he shines like the sun
And he looks so radiant
And he lights up the world

He's the youth of a thousand summers
He's the youth of a thousand summers
Like a sweet bird of youth
Like a sweet bird of youth
In my soul, in my soul, in my soul
In my soul, in my soul, in my soul

In my soul, in my soul, in my soul
In my soul, in my soul, in my soul

He's the king of the mountain
And the clear crystal fountain
He's the saint of the river
He's the ancient of days

He's the youth of a thousand summers
He's the youth of a thousand summers
Like a sweet bird of youth
Like a sweet bird of youth

In my soul, in my soul, in my soul
In my soul, in my soul, in my soul

And he makes you go skipping
And he makes you go dancing
And he gets you in rhythm
And he moves you in song

He's the youth of a thousand summers
He's the youth of a thousand summers
Like a sweet bird of youth
Like a sweet bird of youth
In my soul, in my soul, in my soul
In my soul, in my soul, in my soul
In my soul, in my soul, in my soul
In my soul, in my soul, in my soul

And a sweet bird of youth
In my soul

Professional Jealousy

Professional jealousy can bring down a nation
And personal invasion can ruin a man
Not even his family will understand what's happening
The price that he's paying or even the pain

Professional jealousy started a rumour
And then it extended to be more abuse
What started out as just black propaganda
Was one day seen to be believed as truth

They say the truth is stranger than fiction
But a lie is more deadly than sin
It can make a man very bitter and angry
When he thinks that there's someone, is going to win

Professional jealousy makes others crazy
They think you've got something that they don't have
What they don't understand is it's not that easy
To cover the miles and be where you are

They say that the truth is stranger than fiction
But a lie is more deadly than sin
It can make men bitter, bitter and angry
When they think that someone else is going to win

Professional jealousy makes other people crazy
When they think you've got something that they don't
  have
What they don't understand is it's just not easy
To cover it all and stand where you stand

Professional jealousy makes no exception
It can happen to anyone at any time
The only requirement is knowing what's needed
And then delivering what's needed on time

The only requirement is to know what is needed
In doing the best you know how, deliver on time
The only requirement is to know what is needed
Be best at delivering the product on time

I'm Not Feeling It Anymore

Have to get back, have to get back to base
I need to talk to somebody I can trust
Too many cooks are tryin' to spoil the broth
I can't feel it in my throat, that's all she wrote

I'm not feeling it no more, I'm not feeling it anymore
Not feelin' it no more, not feelin' it anymore

When I was high at the party, everything looked good
I was seein' through rose-coloured glasses
Not seein' the wood for the trees
I started out in normal operation
But I just ended up in doubt
All my drinking buddies, they locked me out

I'm not feelin' it no more, I'm not feelin' it anymore
Not feelin' it no more, I'm tryin' to give you the score

You see me up there baby, I'm on the screen
But I know better now, it's so unreal
If this is success, then something's awful wrong
'Cause I bought the dream and I had to play along

I'm not feelin' it no more, I'm not feelin' it anymore
I'm tryin' to give you the score, I'm not feelin' it no more

We all know that money don't buy you love
You just get a job and somewhere to live
You have to look for happiness within yourself
And don't go chasin' thinkin' that it is somewhere else

I'm not feelin' it no more, I'm not feelin' it anymore
Baby I'm tryin' to give you the score
I'm not feelin' it no more

I was pretending all the time
I was givin' everybody what they wanted
And I lost my peace of mind
And all I ever wanted was simply just to be me
All you ever need is the truth
And the truth will set you free

I'm not feelin' it no more, I'm not feelin' it anymore
I'm tryin' to give you the score, just like I did before
I'm not feelin' it no more, I'm not feelin' it anymore
I'm not feelin' it no more
Baby I'm just trying to give you the score
I'm not feelin' it no more, not feelin' it anymore
Not feelin' it no more
Not feelin' it no more

Some Peace of Mind

You see me on the street, well you guess I'm doing fine
Oh but it's fantasy baby, almost all the time
I've got to get away, by myself
Oh the way it's going, soon be needing help
'Cause I'm just a man, doing the best I can
Don't you understand, I just want some peace of mind

You see me on the stage, doing my job
I learn to do it well, keep on singing the song
But sometimes it gets so lonely out there
When you're on the road and you're going nowhere
Because I'm just a man, oh I ain't got no plans
Don't you understand, I'm just trying to find some peace of mind

I have to stand in line, baby when I'm in the queue
I got to do it all, just the same as you
Got my doubts about it, oh but I try
Oh I make it work with tears in my eyes
Because I'm just a man, only trying to do the best I can
Don't you understand, I want some peace of mind

Oh I'm just a man, baby I ain't got no plan
Oh don't you understand, got to get some peace of mind
Oh got to get, got to get some peace of mind
Oh got to get, got to get some peace of mind
Got to get, get some peace of mind
Get me some, get me some, some peace of mind
Get me some, get me some, peace of mind

Village Idiot

Did you see the lad on the corner?
He was standing drinking wine
Wears his overcoat in the summer
And short sleeves in the wintertime

Takes his holidays down at the bookies
Well he knows how to pick a horse
Village tramping round the countryside
He wears a smile, but he doesn't say much

Village idiot, he's complicated
Village idiot, simple mind
Village idiot, he does know something
But he's just not saying

Don't you know he's onto something?
You can see it, you can see it in his eyes
Sometimes he looks so happy
As he goes strolling by

Oh village idiot, he's complicated
Village idiot, he's got a simple mind
Village idiot, must know something
But he's just not saying

Well you all know he's onto something
You can see it in his eyes
Sometimes he looks so happy
When he goes walking by
Sometimes he looks so happy
When he goes walking by

Sometimes he looks so happy
When he goes walking by

Carrying a Torch

I'm carryin' a torch for you
I'm carryin' a torch
You know how much it costs
To keep carryin' a torch

Flame of love it burns so bright
That is my desire
Keep on liftin' me, liftin' me up
Higher and higher

You're the keeper of the flame
And you burn so bright
Baby why don't we re-connect
Move into the light

I've been going to and fro on this
And I'm still carryin' a torch
You must know how much it's worth
When I'm carryin' a torch

Baby you're the keeper of the flame
And you burn so bright
Why, why, why, why, why, why don't we re-connect
And move on further, into the light

I've been calling you on the phone
'Cause I'm carryin' a torch
I can do it all on my own
'Cause I'm carryin' a torch

I'm carryin' a torch for you, baby

I'm carryin' a torch
You know how much it's worth
Because I'm carryin' a torch

I'm carryin' a torch for you, baby
I'm carryin' a torch
You know how much it's worth
Because I'm carryin' a torch

Pagan Streams

And we walked the pagan streams
And searched for white horses on surrounding hills
We lived where dusk had meaning
And repaired to quiet sleep, where noise abated
In touch with the silence
On Honey Street, on Honey Street

What happened to a sense of wonder?
On yonder hillside, getting dim
Why didn't they leave us, alone?
Why couldn't we just be ourselves?
We could dream, and keep bees
And live on Honey Street

And we walked the pagan streams
In meditation and contemplation
And we didn't need anybody, or anything then
No concepts, being free
And I wanna climb that hillside again, with you
One more time

As the great, great, great, great, great, great, great
Being watches over
And we repair, repair, repair, shhh, repair, shhh, we repair
To Honey Street, to Honey Street

I Need Your Kind of Loving

Well my baby's gone, so's summer
And it brings on a cool night breeze
And I wish we could go walking
By the river, by the shady trees
By the river with the shady trees

Well I love you in the wintertime
Baby when the snow is on the ground
Well I love you in the autumn most of all
When the leaves come tumbling down
When the leaves come tumbling down

Baby I need your kind of loving
For to last my whole life through
Baby I need your kind of loving
You know nobody else will do
You know that nobody else will do

Well I love you in the springtime
When the rippling streams begin to flow
And the weather starts to get a bit warmer
And the grass begins to grow
And the green, green, grass begins to grow

Baby I need your kind of loving
For to last my whole life through
Baby I need your kind of loving
You know that nobody else will do
You know that nobody else will do

Baby I need your kind of loving

For to last my whole life through
Baby I need your kind of loving
You know nobody else will do
You know nobody else will do

Need your kind of loving
Operator, operator
Put me through to my baby now
Operator, put me through to my baby now
To my baby now, to my baby now

Big Time Operators

Well, they told me to come on over
I made my way to New York
And they tried to have me deported
Stop me from getting work
Blacklisted me all over
They were vicious and they were mean
They were big time operators
Baby, on the music business scene

Oh, they looked like politicians
But underneath they were thugs
And they spread malicious rumours
Threatened to have me busted for drugs
They had nothing on me
Oh man, I was really clean
But they were big time operators
On the music business scene

They put a bug in my apartment
To listen in on my calls
I was looking for some motivation
I couldn't find any, any motivation at all
They were very desperate people
Riding in long black limousines
But they were big time operators
On the music business scene

They were glorified by the media
They were heroes who had names
They said that they would bury me
If I didn't play their game

They said I didn't know the score
And that I was young and green
They were big time operators
On the music business scene

Tried to hold me to a phoney contract
I said I didn't agree
Had to get out of their clutches
Had to go underground you see
Now I'm living in another country
But I know exactly just where I've been
Stay away from big time operators
Baby, on the music business scene

Well, baby, big time operators
On the music business scene
Oh baby, big time operators
On the music business scene
Well, full of names and places
Baby, you know who I mean

Perfect Fit

Now baby just lately you've been holding back too much
Your looks and my language, this could be the perfect touch
What you are asking fits with everything on my list
This could be the perfect fit

Tell me that it's madness to want something quite like this
But they don't understand the magic that I can't resist
Oh and wouldn't it be so tragic if everything just went amiss
And this could be the perfect fit

They say no one is perfect, some people might take the piss
And we say we're just friends, come on, tell me what's wrong with this
But I say keep it simple, well we haven't even started yet
And this could be the perfect fit

See that dress you're wearing baby, said it suits you right down to the ground
Tell me where in the world a better loving woman can be found
Well I've searched high and low now and from where you and I sit
And this could be the perfect fit

See that dress you're wearing, suits you right down to the ground
Tell me where in the world a better loving woman can be found
And I've searched high and low now and from where you and I sit
Baby, this could be the perfect fit

Baby, this could be the perfect fit
Come on baby, this could be the perfect fit

Fit, fit, fit, fit, fit, fit, fit, fit, say again
This could be the perfect fit
Fit, fit, fit, fit, fit, fit, fit, fit, fit
This could be the perfect fit

Ancient Highway

There's a small cafe on the outskirts of town
I'll be there when the sun goes down
Where the roadside bends
And it twists and turns
Every new generation
And I'll be praying to my Higher Self
Don't let me down, keep my feet on the ground

There's a roadside jam playin' on the edge of the town
In a town called Paradise near the ancient highway
When the train whistle blows
All the sadness that Hank Williams knows
And the river flows
Call them pagan streams and it spins and it turns
In a factory in a street called Bread in East Belfast
Where Georgie knows best
What it's like to be Daniel in the lion's den
Got so many friends only most of the time

When the grass is high and the rabbit runs
Though it's talkin' to you and I
And every new generation comes to pay
The dues of the organ grinder jam
And the Grinder's Switch of the sacrifice
Everybody made to be rational with understanding
And I'll be praying to my higher self
Oh, don't let me down, keep my feet on the ground

What about all the people living in the nightmare hurt
That won't go away no matter how hard they try
They've got to pay time and time again, time and time again

I'll be praying to my higher self
And I'll be standin' there, where the boats go by
When the sun is sinking way over the hill
On a Friday evening when the sun goes down
On the outskirts of town, I wanna slip away
I wanna slip away, got to get away
And I'll be praying to my higher self
Don't let me down, keep my feet on the ground, don't let me down

You'll be cryin' again, you'll be cryin' again, you'll be cryin' again
By the same wipe the teardrops from your eyes
Have to slip away in the evening when the sun goes down
Over the hill, with a sense of wonder
Everything gonna be right on a Friday evening
All the cars go by all along down
The ancient highway
And I'll be praying, I'll be praying to my higher self
Don't let me down, keep my feet, keep my feet on the ground
Keep my feet on the ground

Travelling like a stranger in the night, all along the ancient highway
Got you in my sights, got you on my mind
I'll be praying in the evening when the sun goes down
Over the mountain, got to get you right in my sight
As the beams from the cars from the overpass
On the ancient highway shine just like diamonds in the night
Like diamonds in the night
I'll be praying to my Higher Self, to my Higher Self
Don't let me down, don't let me down

And you'll be standing there, where the boats go by
Where the boats go by on a Friday evening

Shining your light, shining your light on a Friday evening
Got to slip away, got to slip away down that ancient highway
In a town called Paradise, in a town, in a town
All along, all along that road, all along that road,
All along that road with the trancelike vision
Trancelike vision, trancelike vision
Trancelike vision on my mind

I'll be praying to my higher self, don't let me down, don't let me down
Keep my feet on the ground, keep my feet on the ground,
Keep my feet on the ground
Keep my feet on the ground

Friday evening got to slip away
Watching the view from a car from the overpass
And we're driving down that ancient road
Shining like diamonds in the night, oh diamonds in the night
All along the ancient highway
Got you in my sight, got you in my mind
Got you in my arms and I'm praying, and I'm gonna pray
I'm gonna pray, to my Higher Self, ah don't let me down
Don't let me down, give me the fire, give me the fire

In the Afternoon

The light is fading in the afternoon
Won't you see me baby in my room
There's something that I wanna say to you
Tell me baby am I getting through?
Wanna make, wanna make, wanna make, wanna make
Love to you
Wanna make, wanna make, wanna make, wanna make
Love to you
Wanna make, wanna make, wanna make, wanna make
Love to you
In the afternoon, in the afternoon

The light is fading from across the way
I see you coming baby every day
I see you running, running from across the field
And I wanna know if you feel the same as me
'Cause I wanna make, wanna make, wanna make, wanna
 make
Love to you
Wanna make, wanna make, wanna make, wanna make
Love to you
Wanna make, wanna make, wanna make, wanna make
Love to you
In the afternoon, in the afternoon

The wind is howling baby outside the shack
Train whistle blowin' from across the track
Get on my wavelength, and you set me free
I just wanna be everything you want me to be
Wanna make, wanna make, wanna make, wanna make
Love to you

Wanna make, wanna make, wanna make, wanna make
Love to you
Wanna make, wanna make, wanna make, wanna make
Love to you
In the afternoon, in the afternoon

The moon is sinking way across the trees
I can see my baby but she can't see me
I've got a longing deep within my soul
I have to take it there and let it roll
Wanna make, wanna make, wanna make, wanna make,
  wanna make
Love to you
Wanna make, wanna make, wanna make, wanna make,
Love to you
Wanna make, wanna make, wanna make, wanna make,
Love to you
In the afternoon, make love in the afternoon
Make love in the afternoon

Let it roll
You got me reelin' and a-rockin' and rollin' again
Let it roll
You got me reelin' and a rockin' and rollin' and rollin' again
Oh, I'm rollin' and tumblin', and I'm rollin' and tumblin'
And I'm talkin' all outta my mind baby

Let it roll
You got me reelin' and a-rockin'
And I'm talkin' all outta my mind

I'm talkin' all outta my mind
Make love in the afternoon
Make love in the afternoon
Make love in the afternoon

Rough God Goes Riding

Oh the mud-splattered victims
Have to pay out all along the ancient highway
Torn between half-truth and victimisation
Fighting back with counter attacks

It's when that rough god goes riding
When the rough god goes gliding
When that rough god goes riding
Riding on in

I was flabbergasted by the headlines
People in glasshouses throwing stones
Gaping wounds that will never heal
Now they're moaning like a dog in a manger

It's when that rough god goes riding
When that rough god goes gliding
There'll be nobody hiding
When that rough god comes riding on in

And it's a matter of survival
When you're born with your back against the wall
Won't somebody hand me a bible
Won't you give me that number to call?

When that rough god goes riding
And then that rough god goes gliding
There'll be nobody hiding
When that rough god goes riding on in, riding on in

When that rough god goes riding
When that rough god goes gliding
There'll be nobody hiding
When that rough god goes riding on in
Riding on in

There'll be no more heroes
They'll be reduced to zero
When that rough god goes riding
Riding on in
Riding on in
Riding on in
Riding on in

This Weight

This weight is weighing on my heart
This weight is tearing us apart
This weight is weighing on my soul
And it just won't leave me alone

You know I'm talking about this weight
You know I'm talking about this weight

In the neighbourhood people watching me
Got to move to protect my sanity
Anonymity is all I want you see
You may think it's mediocrity, but

You know I'm talking about this weight
You know I'm talking about this weight

And the Hollywood ain't no good
I would rather be like Robin Hood
If I could only lose this

You know I'm talking about this weight
You know I'm talking about this weight

And this Hollywood ain't no good
I would rather be just like Robin Hood
If I could only lose this

You know I'm talking about this weight
You know I'm talking about this weight

In the very first it was rock 'n' roll
Set me free in body and soul
But this weight is just bringing me down
It's never satisfied every time I go to town
You know I'm talking about this weight

You know I'm talking about this weight
You know I'm talking about this weight
You know I'm talking about this weight

Waiting Game

On a golden autumn day returning
Where each moment never is the same
And pure joy it sometimes comes with patience
When I'm waiting on, waiting game
When I'm waiting on, waiting game

There must be reason for all this inaction
Does it mean that everything must change?
Sometimes I'm looking for perfection
When I'm waiting on, waiting game
When I'm waiting on, waiting game

I am the observer who is observing
I am the brother of the snake
I am the serpent filled with venom
The god of love and the god of hate

There is a presence deep within you
Sometimes they call it higher flame
And the leaves come tumbling down, remember
I'll be waiting on, waiting game
I'll be waiting on, waiting game

I am the observer who is observing
I am the brother of the snake
I am the serpent filled with venom
The god of love and the god of hate

There is a presence deep within you
Some people call it higher power in flame
When the leaves come tumbling down, remember

I'll be waiting on, waiting game
I'll be waiting on, waiting game

Waiting on the waiting game
Waiting on,
Waiting on,
Then I'll come, the waiting game

Piper at the Gates of Dawn

The coolness of the riverbank, and the whispering of the reeds
Daybreak is not so very far away

Enchanted and spellbound, in the silence they lingered
And rowed the boat as the light grew steadily strong
And the birds were silent, as they listened for the heavenly music
And the river played the song

The Wind in the Willows and the Piper at the Gates of Dawn
The Wind in the Willows and the Piper at the Gates of Dawn

The song dream happened and the cloven hoofed piper
Played in that holy ground where they felt the awe and wonder
And they all were unafraid of the great god Pan

And the Wind in the Willows and the Piper at the Gates of Dawn
The Wind in the Willows and the Piper at the Gates of Dawn

When the vision vanished they heard a choir of birds singing
In the heavenly silence between the trance and the reeds
And they stood upon the lawn and listened to the silence

Of the Wind in the Willows and the Piper at the Gates of Dawn
The Wind in the Willows and the Piper at the Gates of Dawn
The Wind in the Willows and the Piper at the Gates of Dawn

It's the Wind in the Willows and the Piper at the Gates of
Dawn
The Wind in the Willows and the Piper at the Gates of Dawn
The Wind in the Willows and the Piper at the Gates of Dawn

It Once Was My Life

There were people on the sidewalks
Strolling down the avenues
They were sitting outside in cafes
We were looking for the muse
Well I was locked in by the system
Where no freedom is the rule
Now I spend all my time just trying
To make it understood

It once was my life, that's what everybody said
All the things I used to do and the people that were friends
I've got to make it mean something at the end of the day
It once was my life, they can't take that away

Trials and tribulations and stupidity still rules
Sometimes it looks like I'm on a ship of fools

It once was my life, when my message was just the street
Then it became something else, and now I'm incomplete
I'm just trying to get back to when
Can somebody please shed some light?
It used to be my life, it used to be uptight

Trials and tribulations and stupidity still rules
Some days it just feels like I'm on a ship of fools

I'm back here on the boards, I can hear the engines roar
Everybody's got to pay, some people got to pay more
Well you can tell the people anything
Spoon feed them anything you like
It used to be so simple, it used to be my life

Now everything is so complicated, just to speak or use the phone
Some people try to use me, just 'cause they don't have their own
Don't know who's round the corner, trying to sell me some more tripe
It used to be my life, it used to be my life
It used to be my life, it used to be my life

The Healing Game

Here I am again
Back on the corner again
Back where I belong
Where I've always been
Everything the same
It don't ever change
I'm back on the corner again
In the healing game

Down those ancient streets
Down those ancient roads
Where nobody knows
Where nobody goes
I'm back on the corner again
Where I've always been
Never been away
From the healing game

Where the choirboys sing
Where I've always been
Sing the song with soul
Baby don't you know
We can let it roll
On the saxophone
Back street jellyroll
In the healing game

Where the homeboys sing
Sing their songs of praise
'Bout their golden days
In the healing game

Sing it out loud
Sing it in your name
Sing it like you're proud
Sing the healing game
Sing it out loud
Sing it in your name
Sing it like you're proud
Sing the healing game

Sing the healing game
Sing the healing game
Sing it in your name
Sing the healing game

Wonderful Remark

How can you stand the silence
That pervades when we all cry?
How can you watch the violence
That erupts before your eyes?

You can't even grab a hold on
When we're hanging oh so loose
You don't even listen to us
When we talk it ain't no use

Leave your thoughtlessness behind you
Then you may begin to understand
Cleave the emptiness around you
With the waving of your hand

That was a wonderful remark
I had my eyes closed in the dark
I sighed a million sighs
I told a million lies to myself, to myself

Now, how can we listen to you
When we know that your talk is cheap?
How can we never question
Why we give more and you keep?

How can your empty laughter
Fill a room like ours with joy?
When you're only playing with us
Like a child does with a toy

How can we ever feel the freedom

Or the flame lit by the spark?
How can we ever come out even
When reality is stark?

That was a wonderful remark
I had my eyes closed in the dark
I sighed a million sighs
I told a million lies to myself, to myself

Listen, how can you tell us something
Just to keep us hanging on
Something that just don't mean nothin'
When we see you, you are gone

Clinging to some other rainbow
While we're standing waiting outside in the cold
Telling us the same sad story
Knowing time is growing old

Touch your world up with some colour
Dream you're swinging on a star
Taste it first then add some flavour
Now you know just who you are

That was a wonderful remark
I had my eyes closed in the dark
I sighed a million sighs
I told a million lies to myself, to myself

Wonderful remark
And that, that was a wonderful remark
I had my eyes closed in the dark
I sighed a million sighs
I told a million lies to myself, to myself

Don't Worry about Tomorrow

Don't worry about tomorrow
That ain't gonna help you none
Don't worry about tomorrow
That ain't gonna help you none
You gotta live and take each day as it comes

It may not be exactly what you're looking for
It may not be exactly what you're looking for
But what you're looking for ain't gonna come walking
Through your front hall door, oh no

So, don't worry about tomorrow
Gotta live each day as it comes
Don't worry about tomorrow
You gotta live each day as it comes
It's the only way you seem to get things done

Try for Sleep

It's four o'clock in the morning, and there's a new full moon
Shining down through the trees
But don't leave the room now, leave it in doubt
Pretend not to know what I'm talking about
I try all night long
I try, I want you to come along

I feel it when you touch me, I'm already wet
But how are you supposed to know what you get
Wake me when it's over, but don't turn on the light
Call me by name, that's alright
I try, all night long,
Ooh, I try to carry on

And, how can you go through, how can you go through
So many changes
Oh, how can you go through, how can you go through
So many changes
It's a family affair, it's a family affair
It's a family affair, it's a family affair, it's a family affair
Try for sleep, why don't you try for sleep
Why don't you try for sleep?

I'm pushin' the river, ready to roll
Oh, I can feel it in my soul
Give me the highlight and leave out the rest
You know what they told me
They said the west is best
I try, all night long, I try to get along with
Will try for sleep, ooh try for sleep
Won't you, oh won't you come along, come along

Try for sleep, try for sleep
I want you to try for sleep
I know you will try, ooh baby
Ooh baby, baby, baby, baby, baby

Drumshanbo Hustle

Lord have mercy! Feel so good
I think I'm gonna work

I was talking to the Judge, just before we left the countryside
Piece of paper in his hand, tryin' to find the way
Tryin' to rip it out, well now I've got it all around
Tore the pages up before they brought the curtain down

I remember the day, the 'Drumshanbo hustle'
When you couldn't hear a bird, it was making not a sound
They were trying to muscle in, an easy way to bring the
  money in
You were puking up your guts
When you looked at the standard contract you just signed

Prostitution on the run, 'cepting when it was soliciting
Tryin' to drain them all dry, got hung up by the rope
Magazines and books, clearly undefinable
Wiped the clean slate, and pulled the rug from underneath
  our feet

I remember the day, the 'Drumshanbo hustle'
When you couldn't hear no birds, 'cos they were making not
  a sound
They were trying to muscle in, the recording and the
  publishing
You were puking up your guts
When you read the standard contract you just signed

New York hooker by the neck, reads your Tarot cards and
  astronomy

Hey, I want to get your stars but don't know your sign
It was taking time to get the message through to it
But will hand down shake you one, and a letter five 'T' rhyme
No sign poker

Oh, remember the day, the 'Drumshanbo hustle'
Couldn't hear a bird, Lord, you couldn't hear no sound
They were trying to muscle in
On the gigs and the recording and the publishing
You were puking up your guts
When you read the standard contract you just signed

You were puking up your guts
When you read the standard contract that you signed
You were puking up your guts
When you read the standard contract you just signed

Goin' Down Geneva

Goin' down Geneva, give me a helping hand
I'm goin' down Geneva, give me a helping hand
It's not easy baby, living on the exile plan

Down on the bottom, down to my new pair of shoes
Down on the bottom, down to my new pair of shoes
I'm down by the lakeside, thinking 'bout my baby blue

Last night I played a gig in Salzburg, outside in the pouring rain
Last night I played a gig in Salzburg, outside in the pouring rain
Flew from there to Montreux and my heart was filled with pain

Look out my window, back at the way things are
Look out my window pane, back at the way things are
Just wonder how, how did things ever get this far

Vince Taylor used to live here, nobody's ever heard of him
Vince Taylor used to live here, but nobody's heard of him, ain't
that a shame
Just who he was, just where he fits in

He was goin' down Geneva, give him a helping hand
He was goin' down Geneva, give him a helping hand
It wasn't easy living on the exile plan

Vince Taylor used to live here, nobody's even heard of him
Vince, Vince Taylor lives here, nobody's even heard of him
Just who he was, just where he fits in

Just who he was, just where he fits in

In the Midnight

In the lonely, dead of midnight
In the dimness of the twilight
By the streetlight, by the lamplight
I'll be around

In the sunlight, in the daylight
When I'm workin', on the insight
And I'm tryin' to keep my game uptight
I'll be around

In your memory, I heard this lonely, lonely music once
In your memory, it's been haunting me ever since

When I'm tryin', tryin' to come down
In my world, my room keeps spinning round
And I'm tryin' to get my feet back on the ground
You'll come around

In my memory, I heard the lonely, lonely music once
In my memory, it's been haunting me ever since

In the lonely, dead of midnight
In the dimness of the twilight
If you meet me, by the lamplight
I'll be around

When I'm tryin' for the come down
And my room keeps spinning round and round
And I'm tryin' to get my feet right back on the ground
You'll come around

When the Leaves Come Falling Down

I saw you standing with the wind and the rain in your face
And you were thinking 'bout the wisdom of the leaves and
their grace
When the leaves come falling down
In September when the leaves, come falling down

And at night the moon is shining on a clear, cloudless sky
But when the evening shadows fall I'll be there by your side
When the leaves come falling down
In September when the leaves come falling down

Follow me down, follow me down, follow me down
To the place beside the garden and the wall
Follow me down, follow me down
To the space before the twilight and the dawn

Oh, the last time I saw Paris in the streets, in the rain
And as I walk along the boulevards with you, once again
And the leaves come falling down
In September when the leaves, leaves come falling down

Follow me down, follow me down, follow me down
To the place between the garden and the wall
Follow me down, follow me down
To the space between the twilight and the dawn

And as I'm looking at the colour of the leaves, in your hand
As we're listening to Chet Baker on the beach, in the sand
When the leaves come falling down,
Oh in September, when the leaves come falling down
Oh when the leaves come falling down

In September when the leaves come falling down

When the leaves come falling down
In September, when the leaves, leaves come falling down

When the leaves come falling down in September, in the rain
When the leaves come falling down

When the leaves come falling down in September, in the rain
When the leaves come falling down

Precious Time

Precious time is slipping away
But you're only king for a day
It doesn't matter to which God you pray
Precious time is slipping away

It doesn't matter what route you take
Sooner or later the heart's going to break
No rhyme or reason, no master plan
No Nirvana, no promised land

Because, precious time is slipping away
You know you're only king for a day
It doesn't matter to which God you pray
Precious time is slipping away

Say que sera, whatever will be
But then I keep on searching for immortality
She's so beautiful but she's going to die some day
Everything in life just passes away

Precious time is slipping away
You know she's only queen for a day
It doesn't matter to which God you pray
Precious time is slipping away

Well this world is cruel with its twists and its turns
Well the fire's still in me and the passion burns
I love her madly 'til the day I die
'Til hell freezes over and the rivers run dry

Precious time is slipping away

You know she's only queen for a day
Doesn't matter to which God you pray because
Precious time is slipping away

Precious time is slipping away
You know you're only king for a day
Doesn't matter to which God you pray
Precious time is slipping away

Precious time is slipping away
You know you're only king for a day
Doesn't matter to which God you pray because
Precious time is slipping away

Golden Autumn Day

Well I heard the bells ringing, I was thinking about winning
In this God forsaken place
When my confidence was well, then I tripped and I fell
Right flat on my face
Now I'm standing erect, and I feel like coming back
And the sun is shining gold
Put a smile on my face, get back in the human race
And get on with the show

And I'm taking in the Indian Summer
And I'm soaking it up in my mind
And I'm pretending that it's paradise
On a golden autumn day, on a golden autumn day
On a golden autumn day, on a golden autumn day
In the wee midnight hour I was parking my car
In this dimly lit town,
I was attacked by two thugs, who took me for a mug
And shoved me down on the ground
And they pulled out a knife, and I fought my way out
As they scarpered from the scene
Well this is no New York street, and there's no Bobby on the
beat
And things just what they seem

And I'm taking in the Indian Summer
And I'm soaking it up in my mind
And I'm pretending that it's paradise
On a golden autumn day, on a golden autumn day
On a golden autumn day, on a golden autumn day

Who would think this could happen in a city like this

Among Blake's green and pleasant hills,
And we must remember as we go through September
Among these dark satanic mills
If there's such a thing as justice I could take them out and
flog them
In the nearest green field
And it might be a lesson to the bleeders of the system
In this whole society

And I'm taking in the Indian Summer
And I'm soaking it up in my mind
And I'm pretending like it's paradise
On a golden autumn day, on a golden autumn day
On a golden autumn day, on a golden autumn day

Golden autumn day

Meet Me in the Indian Summer

Well don't you know
How much I love you
Don't you know
How much I care
It's beyond my comprehension
'Cos I love you on the square

It's not bound by any definition
It isn't written in the stars
It's not limited like Saturn
It isn't ruled by Mercury or Mars

Oh won't you meet me
In the Indian summer?
Where we'll go walking
Down by the weeping willow tree
Won't you meet me
In the Indian summer?
We'll go walking to eternity

It's not modelled by convention
It isn't worshipped like the sun
It's not likened unto any other
And it will never come undone

Well don't you know
That my world is so lonely?
Just like a freight train in the dawn
That's why I need to
Have and hold you
Just to keep me from going wrong

Oh won't you meet me
In the Indian summer?
We'll go walking
By the weeping willow tree
Won't you meet me Lord
In the Indian summer?

We'll go walking to eternity

Won't you meet me
In the Indian summer?
Well before
Those chilly winds do blow
Won't you meet me

In the Indian summer?
Take me way back
To what I know

Oh won't you meet me
In the Indian summer?
We'll go walking
By the weeping willow tree
Oh won't you meet me
In the Indian summer?
We'll go walking to eternity

Whatever Happened to PJ Proby?

Whatever happened to PJ Proby?
Wonder can you fix it Jim
Where the hell do you think is Scott Walker?
My memory's getting so dim

Don't have no frame of reference no more
Not even Screaming Lord Sutch
Without him now there's no Raving Loony Party
Nowadays I guess there's not much

To relate to anymore
Unless you wanna be mediocre
Ain't nothing new under the sun
And the moon and the stars, now chum

I'm making my way down the highway
Still got a monkey on my back
Facing head on and doing it my way
Please can you cut me some slack?

Nothing to relate to anymore
Unless you want to be mediocre
Ain't nothing new under the sun
And the moon and the stars, now chum

Still making my way down the highway
Still got a monkey on my back
Facing head on and doing it my way
Please can you cut me some slack?

All the cards fell so many rounds
Down the road a piece Jack
I saw a bus coming and I had to get on it
I'm still trying to find my way back

Whatever happened to all those dreams a while ago?
Whatever happened way across the sea?
Whatever happened to the way it's supposed to happen?
And whatever happened to me?

The Beauty of the Days Gone By

When I recall just how it felt
When I went walking down by the lake
My soul was free, my heart awake
When I walked down into the town

The mountain air was fresh and clear
The sun was up behind the hill
It felt so good to be alive
On that morning in spring

I want to sing this song for you
I want to lift your spirits high
And in my soul I want to feel
The beauty of the days gone by

The beauty of the days gone by
It brings a longing to my soul
To contemplate my own true self
And keep me young as I grow old

The beauty of the days gone by
The music that we used to play
So lift your glass and raise it high
To the beauty of the days gone by

I'll sing it from the mountain top
Down to the valley down below
Because my cup doth overflow
With the beauty of the days gone by

The mountain glen

Where we used to roam
The gardens there
By the railroad track
Oh my memory it does not lie
Of the beauty of the days gone by

The beauty of the days gone by
It brings a longing to my soul
To contemplate my own true self
And keep me young as I grow old

And keep me young as I grow old
And keep me young as I grow old
And keep me young as I grow old

Man Has to Struggle

Man makes his money and they call him rich
Deep down inside he knows that life's still a bitch
Man tries to keep things but they're taken away
Man has to struggle all the live long day

Man has to sweat and toil his life filled with trouble
Man got to step and fetch it on the double
Man has to work so hard to make it all pay
Man has to struggle all the live long day

Man keeps on moving 'cos he can't keep still
Man has to set his goals and climb up the hill
Man sees the mountains and the deep blue sky
Man has to struggle till the day that he die

Well yes siree Bob, them there's the breaks
That's how it is my friend don't make no mistake

Man has to take some action all of the time
Man by his nature's never satisfied
Man just can't vegetate no matter what they say
Man has to make it all the live long day

Man has to create karma that's the way that it is
Man has to keep on going way beyond his will
Man has to keep on being 'cos there's nothing else
And man just always has to go for himself

Take all the gurus when they meditate
Transcend the mundane into some altered state
You just might get there, but you'll have to pay

Man's got to struggle all the live long day

Well yes siree now Bob, them there's the breaks
That's how it is my friend don't make no mistake

Man has to watch the weather and the food that he eats
Man has to keep fit 'else he's prone to disease
No matter what he does there's stress every which-a-way
Man has to struggle all the live long day

Man is in conflict with his natural self
Man has to suppress his own desires and instincts
Man has to work so hard to keep them at bay
Man has to struggle all the live long day

Man was told that he was born in original sin
By people long ago that were conning him
Man is so out of touch he can't trust himself
But man's still got to win by cunning and stealth

Fast Train

Well you've been on a fast train and it's going off the rails
And you can't come back can't come back together again
And you start breaking down
In the pouring rain
When you've been on a fast train

When your lover has gone away
Don't it make you feel so sad?
And you go on a journey way into the land
And you start breaking down
'Cos you're under the strain
And you jump on a fast train

You had to go on the lam you stepped into no-man's land
Ain't nobody here on your waveband
Ain't nobody gonna give you a helping hand
And you start breaking down
And just go into the sound
When you hear that fast train

And you keep moving on to the sound of the wheels
And deep inside your heart you really know oh, just how it feels
And you start breaking down and go into the pain
Keep on moving on a fast train

You're way over the line
Next thing you're out of your mind
And you're out of your depth
In through the window she crept

Oh there's nowhere to go in the sleet and the snow
Just keep on moving on a fast train

You had to go on the lam stepping in no-man's land
Ain't nobody here on your waveband
Nobody even gonna lend you a helping hand
Oh and you're so alone, can you really make it on your own
Keep on moving on a fast train

Oh going nowhere, except on a fast train
Oh trying to get away from the past
Oh keep on moving keep on moving on a fast train
Going nowhere, across the desert sand, through the barren
   waste
On a fast train going nowhere
On a fast train going nowhere

Whinin' Boy Moan

Drop that coin right into the slot
Get it whether you're ready or not
Let the whinin' boy moan
Let the whinin' boy moan
Let the whinin' boy moan
If you don't know how to do it yourself

Well they call him Mr Jellyroll
It's just the way he rolls his dough
Let the whinin' boy moan
Let the whinin' boy moan
Let the whinin' boy moan
If you don't know how to do it yourself

Well let the whinin' boy moan
If you don't know how to do it yourself
Let the whinin' boy moan
If you don't know how to do it yourself
'Cos he can do it better, better than anyone else
Whine, whine, whine, whine

All the winos down on Market Street
Roll on over to old North Beach
Let the whinin' boy moan
Let the whinin' boy moan
Let the whinin' boy moan
If you don't know how to do it yourself

Well he gonna sing and play for you
Exactly what he's s'pposed to do
Let the whinin' boy moan

Let the whinin' boy moan
Let the whinin' boy moan
If you don't know how to do it yourself
Whine, whine, whine

Let the whinin' boy moan
If you don't know how to do it yourself
Let the whinin' boy moan
If you don't know how to do it yourself
'Cos he can do it better, better than anyone else

Too Many Myths

Too many myths
People just assuming things that aren't true
There's too many myths
Coming between me and you
You might have your name up in lights
But you still have to keep your game uptight

Too many myths
Tell me, tell me how you gonna cope with this
Too many myths
You act like you've never been kissed
You put your name up in lights
And now you gotta keep your game uptight

You got problems
I got problems too
Everybody's gonna think
There must be something wrong with you because

There's just too many myths
Can't you see I'm just trying to stay in the game?
Just too many myths
I'm just trying to maintain
Sure I got my name in lights
But I've still gotta keep my game uptight

You got problems
And I got problems too
But that doesn't necessarily mean that
There's something wrong with you

There's just too many myths
Baby I'm just trying to stay in the game
There's far too many myths
I'm just trying to maintain
I got my name up in lights
But I'm just trying to keep my game uptight

Goldfish Bowl

What will it take for them to leave me alone
Don't they know I'm just a guy who sings songs
I'm not promoting no hit record
And I don't have no TV show
And I don't have no reason to live in the goldfish bowl

I'm just doing my gigs
And I'm on and off the road
Everything I say is not meant to be set in stone
Just because they call me a celebrity
That does not make it true
'Cos I don't believe in the myth people
So why should you

Jazz, Blues & Funk
That's not Rock & Roll
Folk with a beat
And a little bit of Soul
I don't have no hit record
I don't have no TV show
Tell me why should I have to live in this goldfish bowl

Well there's parasites and psychic vampires
Feeding on the public at large
Projecting their shadow onto everyone else
Well the newspaper barons
Are scum of the lowest degree
And they prey on everybody
They prey on you and me

I'm singing Jazz, Blues & Funk

Baby that's not Rock & Roll
Folk with a beat
And a little bit of Soul
I don't have no hit record
I don't have no TV show
So why should I want to live in this goldfish bowl

So why should I have to live in this goldfish bowl?

Little Village

Little village baby, ain't large enough to be a town
From the little village baby, ain't large enough to be a town
Gotta get away from the city
It's gonna bring you down

Heard the voice of the silence, in the evening
In the long cool summer nights
Heard the voice of the silence, in the evening
In the long cool summer night
Telling me not to worry
Everything's gonna be all right

There's only two kinds of truth
Baby let's get it straight from the start
There's only two kinds of truth
Let's get it straight from the start
It's just what you believe
Baby in your head and your heart

Heard the bells ringing
Voices singing soft and low
Heard the bells ringing
Voices were singing soft and low
Way up in the mountain, little village in the snow

Raining in the forest
Just enough to magnetize the leaves
Raining in the forest
Just enough to magnetize the leaves
We'll go walking baby with the moonlight shining down
    through the trees

Little village, way up on the mountainside
Little village baby, way up on the mountainside
Way across the ocean with you by my side

Once in a Blue Moon

Once in a blue moon
Something good comes along
Once in a blue moon
Everything's not going wrong
When you get weary
Beating on the same old gong
Once in a blue moon
Someone like you comes along

Once every once in a while
Something comes along that feels just right
Once every once in a while
Just like switching on an electric light
And sometimes you try till you're blue in the face
But when you get that feeling
Nothing's going to take its place

Once in a blue moon
There's a thing called happiness
It happens when you're in
A state of natural grace

When the wind is blowing
All around the fence
I get that happy feeling
Things start making sense
And you feel so lucky
That you just can't go wrong
Once in a blue moon
Someone like you comes along

Get on with the Show

I just can't seem to take much more of this
Got too much hassle baby and not enough bliss
Got to give these hangers on a miss
'Cos I need some help I just don't get

No one seems to understand what's up
What's up, what's up
So called friends come and go
And things just don't add up
Trying to make my way
Through all this illusion and myth
I don't even have no safety net

Nero fiddled while Rome burnt
Napoleon met his Waterloo
Samson went spare when Delilah cut his hair
But little David slew Goliath too

I'm just trying to get some results
Listen baby I'm not trying to start my own cult
Please tell me something that I don't know
I just wanna get on with the show

Nero fiddled while Rome burnt
Napoleon met his Waterloo
Samson went spare when Delilah cut his hair
But little David slew Goliath too

You'd think some program might do the trick
Let me tell you this wall of fog
Is just too thick

I thought of everything but the whip
But baby nobody on my ship is up to it

I'm just trying to get some results, some results
I'm not trying to start my own cult, no
Just tell me something I don't know
I just wanna get on with the show

I just wanna get on with the show
Just tell me something that I don't know
I just wanna get on with the show
And if it don't work then let it go

Fame

Oh fame, they've taken everything and twisted it
Oh fame they say
You never could have resisted it
What's in a name?
When everybody's jaded by fame

Oh fame again
The press has gone and made another mess of it
Oh just because they've got
So much invested in it
But they say you're to blame it's your own fault
'Cos you got mixed up in fame

Oh no don't believe all that old Andy Warhol guff
It takes a lot more than 10 or 15 minutes
That's just not enough
To qualify you for fame

You went beyond the boundaries of sanity
And every day you defy
All the laws of gravity
You ain't got no shame
'Cos you're just addicted to fame

Oh no don't you buy none of that old Andy Warhol stuff
It takes a lot more than 10 or 15 minutes
That's just not enough
To qualify you for fame

They're already setting up your own Watergate
Oh fame, that stalker out there is just filled with hate

You'll never be the same
'Cos everyone's corrupted by fame

Oh fame, you took away all my humanity
Oh fame got to fight
Every second of the day for my dignity
It's a spectator's game
And there ain't nothin' fair about fame

Oh fame
Oh fame say it again
Oh fame say it again
Fame
They say you're to blame
'Cos you got mixed up in fame

Celtic New Year

If I don't see you through the week
See you through the window
See you next time that we're talking on the telephone
And if I don't see you in that Indian summer
Then I want to see you further on up the road

I said, oh won't you come back?
Have to see you my dear
Won't you come back in the Celtic New Year?
In the Celtic New Year

If I don't see you when I'm going down Louisiana
If I don't see you when I'm down on Bourbon Street
If you don't see me when I'm singing 'Jack O' Diamonds'
If you don't see me when I'm on my lucky streak

Oh, I want you, want you to come on back
I've made it very clear
I want you to come back home in the Celtic New Year
Celtic New Year

If I don't see you when the bonfires are burning, burning
If I don't see you when we're singing the Gloriana tune
If I've got to see you when it's raining deep inside the forest
I got to see you at the waning of the moon

Said oh, won't you come on back?
Want you to be of good cheer
Come back home on the Celtic New Year

Celtic New Year, Celtic New Year

Celtic New Year
In the Celtic New Year
In the Celtic New Year

Come on home, come on home
Come on home, come on home
In the Celtic New Year
In the Celtic New Year

Magic Time

Don't lose the wonder in your eyes
I can see it right now when you smile
Let me go back, for a while
Let me go back, for a while
To that magic time

You can call it nostalgia, I don't mind
Standing on that windswept hillside
Listenin' to the church bells chime
Listen to the church bells chime
In that magic time

Oh the road it never ends
Good to see you my old friend
Once again we sit right down and share the wine

Shivers up and down my spine
It's a feeling so divine
Let me go back for a while
Got to go back for a while
To that magic time

Oh the road it never ends
Good to see you my old friend
Once again we'll sit down and share the wine

Got to go back
And we'll go back in your prime
The sun is gonna shine
When we go back for a while
When we go back for a while

To that magic time

Don't lose the wonder in your eyes
It's right there when you smile
Got to go back, for a while
Got to go back, for a while
To that magic time

Call it nostalgia, I don't mind
Standing on that windswept hillside
Listenin' to the church bells chime
Listenin' to the church bells chime
In that magic time

If we go back, for a while
Let me go back, for a while
To that magic time

Blue and Green

Blue and green
Well my song is blue and green
Blue and green
Well my song is blue and green
What I say
Baby, baby what I mean

Blue up in the sky
And Mother Nature's green
Don't have to wonder why
Just taking in this country scene
Driving through the land
Understanding blue and green

Sometimes it feels like baby
That I've been seeing red
Sometimes it feels like baby
That I've been seeing red
Woke up early one morning
Mr Blue and Green was standing round my bed

Blue and green
That's the colours that I see
Blue, blue, blue, blue, blue and green
But that doesn't mean that you should envy me
Hear what I say, I say what I mean
Oh blue and green

Early in the morning
Sometimes I feel I'm seeing red
Early in the morning

Well I feel I'm seeing red
Gotta blues all in my breakfast
And green all in my head

Blue blue blue blue blue blue blue blue
Blue and green
Sky is blue
And Mother Nature's green
Keep on driving through the land
Taking in the country scene

Behind the Ritual

Drinking wine in the alley, drinking wine in the alley
Making time, drinking that wine
Out of my mind in the days gone by

Making time with Sally, drinking that wine
In the days gone by, talking all out of my mind
Drinking that wine, talking all out of my mind

Spin and turning in the alley, spin and turning in the alley
Like a Whirling Dervish in the alley, drinking that wine
Drinking wine, making time in the days gone by

Boogie-woogie child in the alley
Drinking that wine, making time, talking all out of my mind
Drinking wine in the days gone by, behind the ritual

Behind the ritual, behind the ritual
In the days gone by, drinking that wine
Making time, drinking that wine way back in time

Spin and turn and rhyme in the alley
Spin and turning, making it rhyme, talking all out of my mind
Talking that jive, drinking that wine in the days gone by

Drinking wine in the alley, drinking that wine
Making time, talking all out of my mind
Drinking that wine making time in the alley

Behind the ritual, behind the ritual
You find the spiritual, you find the spiritual

Behind the ritual in the days gone by
Drinking wine in the alley, drinking wine in the alley
Making time, talking all out of my mind
Drinking that wine in the days gone by, days gone by

Spin and turn talking that jive
Spin and turn talking that jive all out of our minds
Drinking that sweet wine
Making time, making time in the days gone by

Behind the ritual, behind the ritual
Behind the ritual, behind the ritual
Drinking that wine making time in the days gone by

Behind the ritual, making time in the days gone by

In the days gone by, in the days gone by
Drink that wine, making time
Getting high in the days gone by, drinking that wine

Getting high behind the ritual
Getting high behind the ritual
Drinking that wine in the days gone by

Behind the ritual, behind the ritual
Behind the ritual, behind that spiritual
In the days gone by drinking that wine and getting high

So high behind the ritual, so high behind the ritual
So high in the days gone by
Drinking that wine making time, making time

Stretching time, stretching time
Drinking that wine, stretching time
Stretching time in the days gone by behind the ritual

Behind the ritual
Behind the ritual

How Can a Poor Boy?

Had my congregation, had my flock
When I was a shepherd of men
Chased the wild goose, chased the pot of gold
Chased the rainbows end

How can a poor boy deliver this message to you?
How can a poor boy? You don't believe anything that's true

Had my rise, had my downfall
Now I'm gonna rise up again
Had my degrees, my initiations
Not speaking to the profane

How can a poor boy get this message to you?
How can a poor boy when you don't believe a thing that's true?

I've been anointed, been appointed
Even been magnified
Spied a chapel all of gold
The priest was laying down with the swine

How can a poor boy get a little message to you?
How can a poor boy when you don't believe anything is true?
How can a poor boy get this message through to you?
How can a poor boy when you don't believe a single thing is true?

Watch the illusion of false security
Play of the shadows that move

Tell me what evil lurks in the hearts of men
Only the shadow knows

How can a poor boy get this message to you?
How can a poor boy when you don't believe a thing that's
  true, for you
When you don't believe a thing, nothing that's true for you
How can a poor boy ever get next to you?

Open the Door (to Your Heart)

Open the door to your heart
Open the door to your soul
Get back in the flow
Open the door to your heart

Money doesn't make you fulfilled
Money's just to pay the bills
It's need not greed
Open the door to your heart

You've got eyes to see
And ears to hear
Then why don't you quit
Crying in your beer my dear

If nobody gets what they want
Tell me what's the use in that
Everybody just gets fat
Open the door to your heart

Backbiters always make mistakes
If you want to get an even break
Think of everything that's at stake
Open the door to your heart

Don't you think I know who my enemies are?
Their slip is showing and the door is ajar
Well this time they pushed me too far
Open the door to your heart

If you've got eyes to see

And ears to hear
You better quit, quit
Crying in your beer my dear

If you can't hear the song you're wrong
I've been around too long
Just listen to the words that's all
Open the door to your heart
Open the door to your heart
Open the door to your soul
Got to get back in the flow
Open the door to your heart

Come on
Open the door to your heart
Open the door to your soul
Get back in the flow
Open the door to your heart

Come on, come on, come on
Come on, come on, come on

Open the door to your heart
Open the door to your soul
Got to get back in the flow now
Open the door to your heart

Come on, come on, come on,
Come on, come on, come on

Open the door to your heart

Goin' Down to Monte Carlo

Goin' down to Monte Carlo about 25K from Nice
Goin' down to Monte Carlo about 25K from Nice
Got to get myself together, gotta get my head some peace

Sartre said that hell is other people, I believe that most of
them are
Sartre said hell is other people, I believe that most of them
are
Well their pettiness amazes me, even after I'm gone this far

Goin' down to Monte Carlo 25K from Nice
Goin' down to Monte Carlo 'bout 25K from Nice
Gotta get my head together, gotta get my head some peace.

Playing in the background some kind of phoney pseudo jazz
Playing in the background in the restaurant, some kind of
phoney pseudo jazz
I don't care I'm trying to get away from people, that are
trying to drive me mad

After everything I've worked for, not goin' to throw
everything away
After everything I worked so hard for, I'm not goin' to give it
all away
I just need to take a rain check, I can live to fight another day

Goin' down to Monte Carlo, 25K from Nice
Goin' down, goin' down to Monte Carlo, still about 25K
from Nice
Got to get my head showered, got to find some release

Born to Sing

Man can be king
Seems to have everything
But it comes with a sting
When you were born to sing

Reason doesn't walk in
It's not done on a whim
Passion's everything
When you were born to sing

Feeling good
Singing the blues
It ain't easy
Keep on paying dues

When it gets to the part
Well let's not stop and start
Deep down in your heart
You know you were born to sing

When you came in
No original sin
You were a king
Because you were born to sing

Reason doesn't walk in
It's not done on a whim
Passion's everything
When you were born to sing

Lord, feeling good

Singing the blues
Keep on keeping on
Paying them dues

When it comes to the part
Well let's not stop and start
Deep down in your heart
Baby you were born to sing

When it gets to the part
When the band starts to swing
Then you know everything
'Cause you were born to sing

When it gets to the part
When the band starts to swing
Then you know everything
'Cause you were born to sing

Close Enough for Jazz

No use feeling sad
No use staying mad
Better when you're glad
You can be there in a heartbeat
When it's close enough for jazz
Close enough for jazz

Be glad with what you have
Even if it's half
Empty in the glass
If there's room to move your elbows
Then it's close enough for jazz
Close enough for jazz

When you're not in a hurry
When things may turn around
Never give in to worry
Try looking up not down, don't frown

Close enough for jazz
Is it Persil is it Daz?
Well it doesn't really matter
When it's better on the inside
And it's close enough for jazz
Close enough for jazz
Close enough for jazz
Close enough for jazz

Retreat and View

From my retreat and view
Make my own break through
And I might see things new
From my retreat and view

There's visions to behold
Treasures to unfold
Home away from home
From my retreat and view

Well the higher you go
The more that you know you can find
Like a memory that's there
Stuck in the back of your mind

There's bargains of the soul
Dreams that do unfold
Now I know it's true
From my retreat and view

There's bargains of the soul
Treasures to behold
Some time to start anew
From my retreat and view

From my retreat and view
Got to make my own break through
So I can see things new
From my retreat and view

High up on the mountainside

From my retreat and view
The place to satisfy
From my retreat and view

From my retreat and view
Got to make my own break through
So I can see things new
From my retreat and view

Pagan Heart

My pagan heart
My pagan soul
Got to move on to the crossroads
Got to go to the arcadian groves
Got to move to the crossroads
Down by the crossroads, crossroads

My pagan heart
My pagan soul
Got to go to the holy wood
When the sun is good, to the holy wood
You take it in, it's under your skin
It tastes like wine
In the evening time
Down by the crossroads
Down by the crossroads

My pagan heart
My pagan soul
Down, down, down, down
Down by the arcadian groves
Down, down, down, down,
Down by arcadian groves
By the roads
By the roads
My pagan heart
My pagan soul

My pagan heart
My pagan soul
I got to go down, by the crossroads

The moon is rising
In the evening time
By the crossroads, crossroads
My pagan heart
My pagan soul

Down down down down
Down by the arcadian grove
Down down down down
Down by the arcadian grove
Got to go down by the crossroads, crossroads
My pagan heart
My pagan soul
My pagan heart
My pagan soul
Got to go down by the crossroads, crossroads
Pagan heart
My pagan soul
Got to go down
To the crossroads

I look at the sun, I take it in
It's under my skin
Pagan heart
Pagan soul
Pagan heart
Pagan soul
I've got to know
I got to know
Pagan heart
Pagan soul
Put a spell on you
Put a spell on you
Down by the crossroads
My pagan heart

My pagan soul
Pagan heart
Pagan soul
Put a spell on you
Down by the crossroads
When the moon was new
When the moon was new
Put a spell on you

In Tiburon

Across the bay the fog is lifting
And I am here in Tiburon
That's what she said
When she was sitting looking out at the Golden Gate
In the morning dawn

Across the bay in San Francisco
Where City Lights and Ferlinghetti stay
North Beach alleyways and cafes
Kerouac and Ginsberg
Gregory Corso and Neal Cassady all held sway

Vince Guaraldi would play 'Cast Your Fate to the Wind' in
 the distance
Lenny Bruce got busted at 'The Hungry Eye'
The 'No-Name Bar' down in Sausalito
Across the street where Chet Baker used to play

My heart was beating on the hillside
Near Belvedere and Tiburon
I need to take you back, back down to 'Frisco
Now we need each other, need each other to lean on

Vince Guaraldi would play 'Cast Your Fate to the Wind'
and we'd listen
In the evening across the way
Chet Baker would play down at the Trident
With his horn he blew everybody away

The Cliff House down at the Sea Rock Hotel
Foghorns blowing all night long till dawn

Geary Street culchies left their homeland a long while ago
Some have stayed, but others not for so long

My heart was beating on the hillside
Near Belvedere and Tiburon
Take you back down to San Francisco
Now we need each other more than ever to lean on
Now we need each other more than ever, more than ever to lean on

Lean on me
Lean on
Now we need each other more than ever to lean on

Back to City Lights, City Lights
North Beach and Broadway
We need each other

We need each other to lean on

Back to City Lights and North Beach
North Beach and Broadway
We need each other, need each other to lean on

Across the bay in Tiburon
Across the bay in Tiburon
And across the bay in Tiburon
And across the bay in Tiburon

Look Beyond the Hill

When your troubles are a burden let your mind be still
Wait until the clouds start moving way beyond the hill

Can't you see the sky is bluer up upon the ridge
Just don't let the green grass fool you, look beyond the hill

Sometime it don't rhyme, seem to have your fill
Got to get your house in order in line with your will

Tomorrow is another day to go in for the kill
You can have a change of heart now
Look beyond the hill

You got to look beyond the hill
You got to look beyond the hill

Memory Lane

It's autumn time, going on November
I view the leaves in all their splendour
Is it déjà vu, I just can't remember
I stop a while and take in the scene

I stop a while and ask a stranger
Is this the place that was once called Memory Lane?
I don't know where I am or what I'm after
I'm stuck here again back on Memory Lane

Now the leaves are falling and it's coming on to winter
Nights keep getting shorter and shorter every day
One sign up ahead says 'danger'
Another one says 'stop'
One says 'yield this way'

And it swerves and moves around the corners
And there's flashing lights up ahead 'round the bend
Road curves and twists and turns and twists and turns and
 wanders
'Til you get, 'til you get to the very end

Now I'm back here again with more questions than answers
And I'm standing in the pouring rain
There's something moving, moving in the shadows
And it's getting dark now up on Memory Lane

I stop a while and ask some strangers
Is this the place that was once called Memory Lane?
I don't know where I am, don't know what I'm after
I'm stuck here back up on Memory Lane

I stop a while and ask some strangers
Is this the place that once was called Memory Lane?
Don't know where I am right now or what I'm after
I'm stuck here up, stuck on Memory Lane
I'm stuck here up, back on Memory Lane
I'm stuck here back up on Memory Lane
I'm stuck here back, back up on Memory Lane

The Pen Is Mightier than the Sword

You've got to live by the pen 'cause it's mightier than the sword
You've got to live by the pen 'cause it's mightier than the sword
Every man is me every man is you
I can't tell you what you've got to do
You've got to live by the pen, it's mightier than the sword

You've got to live by the pen 'cause it's mightier than the sword
You've got to live by the pen 'cause it's mightier than the law
Every man is me every man is you
I can't tell you what you have to do
You've got to live by the pen 'cause it's mightier than the sword

You've got to live by the pen 'cause it's mightier than the law
You've got to live by the pen 'cause of what you saw
Every man is me every man is you
I can't tell you what you're supposed to do
I've got to live by the pen 'cause it's mightier than the sword

I've got to live by the pen 'cause it's mightier than the sword
I've got to live by the pen 'cause it's mightier than the sword
Every man is me every man is you
But I can't tell you what you have to do
I've got to live by the pen 'cause it's mightier than the sword

They're gonna get burned 'cause they're playing with fire
They're gonna get caught 'cause somebody is a liar
Every man is me every man is you

I can't tell you what you're supposed to do
You've got to live by the pen 'cause it's mightier than the sword

I've got to live by the pen 'cause it's mightier than the sword
I've got to live by the pen 'cause it's mightier than the sword
Every man is me every man is you
I can't tell you what you're supposed to do
I've got to live by my pen 'cause it's mightier than the law
I've got to live by my pen 'cause it's mightier than the sword
I've got to live by my pen 'cause it's mightier than the sword

Transformation

Gonna be a transformation in your heart and soul
Gonna be a transformation baby now that you know
Get used to righteousness when it makes you feel whole
Gonna be a transformation baby down in your soul

Remember when we were downhearted didn't have nowhere
 to go
And the wisdom of insecurity just knowing that we know
Then something starts happening feel like you're on a roll
Gonna be a transformation baby down in your soul

God's like a river keeps on wanting to flow
Keeps on advancing with the wisdom you know
Time has a rhythm when the love is the law
Love is forever baby down in your soul

Gonna be a transformation baby down in your soul
Gonna be a transformation now that you know
Get used to righteousness 'cause it makes you feel whole

Gonna be a transformation down in your soul
Gonna be a transformation down in your soul
Gonna be a transformation baby now that you know

Get used to righteousness 'cause it makes you feel whole
Gonna be a transformation right down in your soul

Gonna be a transformation, down in your soul
Gonna be a transformation, down in your soul

Broken Record

Baby, stall the gate for me
Take me, lift me out of my misery
Lift my spirit up, and set me free

When things are driving me insane
Let me hear that same refrain
Over and over and over
And over and over and over and over again

Take it to the break
Don't make any mistake
For goodness sake
Have to stay awake

Broken record, broken record, broken record
Broken record, broken record, broken record
Broken record, broken record, broken record
Broken record, broken record, broken record
Broken record, broken record

Take it to the break
Make no mistake
Stay awake
Whatever it takes

Broken record, broken record, broken record
Broken record, broken record, broken record
Broken record, broken record, broken record
Broken record, broken record, broken record
Broken record, broken record, broken record

Broken record, broken record, broken record
Broken record, broken record, broken record
Broken record, broken record, broken record
Broken record, broken record, broken record
Broken record, broken record

5am Greenwich Mean Time

Well I'm thinking about my people and the love that we once had
Well I'm thinking about my people and the love that we once had
But I don't understand how everything got so bad

Well I'm walking in the morning and I'm talking all to myself
Well I'm walking in the morning and I'm talking all to myself
And it's 5am and its Greenwich Mean Time

Well I'm wondering what happened to my baby child
And I'm wondering what happened to my baby child
Gonna drive me crazy, gonna drive me wild

Well I'm walking in the morning and I'm walking all by myself
Well I'm walking in the morning and I'm talking all by myself
Well it's 5am and I think I'm gonna need some help

Well I'm walking up the hillside and I'm trying to catch the bus on time
Well I'm walking up the hillside and I'm trying to catch my bus on time
You see you do anything to keep everybody satisfied

And I'm wondering what happened to my baby child
And I'm wondering what happened to my baby child
I'm walking in the morning and it's 5am Greenwich Mean Time

Yeah, thinking about my people and the love that we once had

Well I'm thinking about my people and the love that we once had
Well I don't understand how everything just got so bad

I'm walking in the morning and I'm talking all by myself
Well I'm walking in the morning and I'm talking all by myself
It's 5am and I think I'm gonna need some help

I'm walking in the morning, Greenwich Mean Time
I'm walking in the morning, Greenwich Mean Time
It's 5am and I think I'm gonna lose my mind

Well I'm walking in the morning and it's 5am Greenwich Mean Time

Ain't Gonna Moan No More

Oh oh oh ain't gonna moan no more
Oh oh oh ain't gonna moan no more
Ain't no wolf at my door
Ain't gonna moan no more

From the Old Groaner to the deep deep blues
Muddy Waters and John Lee too
From the master of vocalese
Jon Hendricks sang it with ease
Ain't gonna moan no more

Satchmo chose playin' the clown
It didn't stop him layin' it down
He chose to smile instead of frown
He kept playin' his gigs and movin' from town to town

No time to frown
Ain't gonna moan today
Goin' to town gonna make my day
Do my best to create all the better space
Ain't gonna moan no more, man
Around this place

Willie The Shake said that 'life is what you make it'
Somebody else said, 'fake it till you make it'
Well I feel much better when my feet are touchin' the ground
I get hip to the tip when I hear that lonesome sound

Some people's down
Someone else is upbeat
Transform the norm, tryin' to make it sweet

When you know things are happening
Well it just can't be beat
When you know the score
You don't have to moan no more

Oh oh oh ain't gonna moan no more
Oh woah ain't gonna moan no more
Ain't no wolf at my door
Ain't gonna moan no more

Oh oh oh

Ain't no wolf at my door
Ain't gonna moan no more
Oh oh oh hey, ain't gonna moan no more
Oh oh oh ain't gonna moan no more
When you know the score
Don't have to moan no more

Love Is Hard Work

Love is hard work that's a fact
Think you're moving forward but it's setback after setback
Love is hard work that's an actual fact
Think you're moving forward but it's setback after setback

No such thing as standard no such thing as norm
Think you know it then your sanity is gone
Love is hard work baby, that's a fact
Think you're moving forward but it's setback after setback

Some people say love's a mugs' game
Feel like leaving on the midnight train
Trying to play your part what stage does it become fun?
Love is hard work now it's got me on the run

Love is hard work baby that's a fact
Two steps forward and three steps back
Love is hard work now now, man that's a fact
Think you're moving but it's setback after setback

Love is hard work baby, that's a fact
Two steps forward and three steps back
Love is hard work, that's an actual fact
When you think you're moving it's setback after setback

Some people say love's a mugs' game
Feel like leaving on the midnight train
But I've got to double back, double back
Love is hard work now baby, that's a fact

Love is hard work, love is hard work

Love is hard work, baby that's a fact
When you think you're moving it's setback after setback

Spirit Will Provide

Spirit will provide beyond the lie
Spirit will provide beyond the why
Spirit will provide, spirit will provide

Let go, let go then spirit will provide
Change your thought and it will change your mind
Spirit will provide, spirit will provide

It's no mystery when you can see clearly
Vibrating at a higher frequency
Fill your purpose as you go about life daily
Understanding what it means to clearly see

Spirit will provide when you feel down
Plug into don't buy what's goin' round
Spirit will provide, spirit will provide

It's no mystery when you can see clearly
Vibrating, vibrating at the higher frequency
Fulfilling your purpose as you go about life daily
Understanding what it means to clearly see

Spirit will provide now dry your eyes
Spirit will provide now don't you cry
Spirit will provide, spirit will provide
Spirit will provide, spirit will provide

Spirit will provide, spirit will provide
Spirit will provide, spirit will provide

The Prophet Speaks

When the prophet speaks
Mostly no one listens
When the prophet speaks and no one hears
Only those who have ears to listen
Only those who are trained to hear

Come closer now
I'll tell you with a whisper
Close and I will whisper it in your ear
What big ears you've got when you get the details
Do you understand
Do I make it clear

When the prophet speaks
And no one listens
When the prophet speaks
Mostly no one hears
Only those that are trained to listen
Only those who have ears to hear

When the prophet speaks and no one listens
Baby, don't you have no fear
You gotta get the truth of what is happening
When the prophet speaks, have to make it clear
Come closer now, and I will whisper
Whisper the secret in your ear
What big ears you've got when you get all the details
Do you understand, do I make myself clear

When the prophet speaks you've gotta listen
When the prophet speaks you've got to get the truth

When the prophet speaks don't need no explanation
When the prophet speaks, have to make it move

Prophet speaks no one listens
When the prophet speaks mainly nobody hears
Only those that are trained to listen
Only those who have ears to hear

Acknowledgements

Many thanks to Dan Papps at Faber for all his assistance in bringing this edition together. Sincere thanks to John Cooper Clarke, Eamonn Hughes and Kerry Adamson.

Index of Titles and First Lines

Song titles are in italic; first lines are in roman

5am Greenwich Mean Time, 437–8

Across the bay the fog is lifting, 427
Ain't Gonna Moan No More, 439–40
Alan Watts Blues, 137–8
All Saints Day, 163
All that trouble, all that grief, 198
All the men would turn their head, 183
All the people were waiting for Crazy Face, 46
Among the rolling hills, 89
Ancient Highway, 350–2
And all my love come down, 60
And as we walked, 273
And I shall stroll the merry way and jump the hedges first, 239
And I take you down to the burning ground, 178
And It Stoned Me, 241–2
And she moves on the solid ground, 312
And the caravan is on its way, 244
And the Healing Has Begun, 91–3
And we walked the pagan streams, 343
And we'll walk down the avenue again, 91
And when heart is open, 309
As you brush your shoes, 257
Astral Weeks, 236–8
Autumn Song, 264–6

Baby, stall the gate for me, 435
The Back Room, 30–2
Bad or Good, 227–8
Beautiful Vision, 108–9
Beautiful vision, 108
The Beauty of the Days Gone By, 386–7
Behind the Ritual, 411–13
Big Time Operators, 346–7
Blue and Green, 409–10
Blue and green, 409
Blue Money, 49–50
Born to Sing, 419
Boy and his dog, 262
Brand New Day, 44–5
Bright Side of the Road, 87–8
Broken Record, 435–6
Brown Eyed Girl, 21–2
Bulbs, 73–4
Burning Ground, 178–9
By the mansion on the hillside, 194
By the side of the tracks where the train goes by, 246

Call of the wildest, it's got the best of you, 176
Caravan, 244–5
Carrying a Torch, 341–2
Celtic New Year, 405–6
Celtic Ray, 104–5
Chamois cleaning all the windows, 62
Checkin' It Out, 385–6
Chop that wood, 330
Choppin' Wood, 196–7
Cleaning Windows, 112–13
Close Enough for Jazz, 421
Cold Wind in August, 80–1
Come Here My Love, 76
Come here, my love, 76
Come Running, 246–7
Comfort You, 75
Coming back from Downpatrick, 147
Coney Island, 147

Contacting My Angel, 322
Contacting my angel, contacting my angel, 322
The coolness of the riverbank, and the whispering of the reeds, 361
Copycats ripped off my songs, 317
Could You, Would You, 229
Could you, would you, hold me in your arms, 229
Crazy Face, 46
Crazy Love, 243
Cry for Home, 117–18
Cul-de-Sac, 77

Dadada da da da, dada da da da, 56
Daring Night, 325–7
Days Like This, 175
Did Ye Get Healed?, 139–40
Did you ever hear about the great deception?, 71
Did you see the lad on the corner?, 339
Domino, 251–2
Don't lose the wonder in your eyes, 407
Don't want to discuss it, 251
Don't Worry about Tomorrow, 369
Don't worry about tomorrow, 369
Down on Cyprus Avenue, 35
Down the mystic avenue I walk again, 110
Drinking wine in the alley, drinking wine in the alley, 411
Drop that coin right into the slot, 392
Drumshanbo Hustle, 372–3
Dweller on the Threshold, 106–7

End of the Land, 209
Enlightenment, 330–1
The Eternal Kansas City, 279–80
Everybody's got some soul, 227
Everyone, 250
Excuse me, do you know the way to Kansas City?, 279

Fair Play, 269–70
Fair play to you, 269
Fame, 403–4
Fast Train, 390–1
The fields are always wet with rain, 127
Fill me my cup, 18
Fire in the Belly, 176–7
Flamingos Fly, 283–4
Foghorns blowing in the night, 151
Foreign Window, 130–1
Friday's Child, 230–1
From my retreat and view, 422
From the ancient sun to the old hearth stove, 303
From the dark end of the street, 87
From the North to the South, 230
Full Force Gale, 297–8

Get on with the Show, 401–2
Give Me My Rapture, 321
Gloria, 16–17
Go for a ride, 283
Goin' Down Geneva, 374
Goin' down Geneva, give me a helping hand, 374
Goin' Down to Monte Carlo, 418
Goin' down to Monte Carlo about 25K from Nice, 418
Golden Autumn Day, 380–1
Goldfish Bowl, 396–7
Gonna be a transformation in your heart and soul, 434
Got to Go Back, 125–6
The Great Deception, 71–2
Gypsy, 58–9

Had my congregation, had my flock, 414
Half a mile from the county fair, 241
Hard Nose the Highway, 68
Haunts of Ancient Peace, 311
Have I Told You Lately that I Love You?, 145
Have I told you lately that I love you?, 145

Have to get back, have to get back to base, 336
Have to toe the line, I've got to make the most, 157
The Healing Game, 365–6
Heart and soul, 116
Here comes Sue and she looks crazy, 163
Here I am again, 365
He's the youth of a thousand summers, 332
Hey, kids, dig the first takes, 68
Hey, where did we go, days when the rains came, 21
Higher Than the World, 114–15
High Summer, 194–5
How Can a Poor Boy?, 414–15
How can you stand the silence, 367
How sweet that joyous sound, 281
Hungry for Your Love, 291–2
Hymns to the Silence, 164–5

I can hear her heart beat from a thousand miles, 243
I dreamed you paid your dues in Canada, 248
I Forgot that Love Existed, 134
I forgot that love existed, trouble in my mind, 134
I just can't seem to take much more of this, 401
I Need Your Kind of Loving, 344–5
I saw you from a foreign window, 130
I saw you standing with the wind and the rain in your face, 376
I waited for you, 80
I walked in my greatcoat down through the days of leaves, 314
I wanna comfort you, 75
I wanna know did you get the feeling, 139
I Wanna Roo You, 259–60
I want you to be around, 55
I Will Be There, 261
I'd Love to Write Another Song, 323
I'd love to write another song, 323
If I don't see you through the week, 405
If I Ever Needed Someone, 255–6
If I ventured in the slipstream, 236
If You and I Could Be As Two, 225–6
I'll be waiting, 117
I'm a dweller on the threshold, 106
I'm a songwriter and I know just where I stand, 174
I'm carryin' a torch for you, 341
I'm hungry for your love, 291
I'm kicking off from centrefield, 73
I'm Not Feeling It Anymore, 336–7
I'm stranded at the edge of the world, 205
I'm Tired Joey Boy, 324
I'm tired Joey boy, 324
I'm walkin' down the street, 287
In haunts of ancient peace, 311
In the Afternoon, 353–4
In the back room, in the back room, 30
In the cul-de-sac, 77
In the daring night, 325
In the Days Before Rock 'n' Roll, 153–4
In the Garden, 127–8
In the lonely, dead of midnight, 375
In the Midnight, 375
In Tiburon, 427–8
Inarticulate speech, inarticulate speech of the heart, 313
Inarticulate Speech of the Heart, 313
Into the Mystic, 43
Irish Heartbeat, 141–2
It Fills You Up, 78–9
It Once Was My Life, 363–4
It was on a Sunday and the autumn leaves were on the ground, 225
It's autumn time, going on November, 430
It's four o'clock in the morning, and there's a new full moon, 370
I've been searching a long time, 135

I've been walking by the river, 160
I've Been Workin', 47–8
I've been workin', 47
I've given you my heart and my soul, 207

Jackie Wilson Said (I'm in Heaven When You Smile), 56–7
Joe Harper Saturday Morning, 33–4
Joyous Sound, 281–2
Just a closer walk with Thee, 158
Justin, gentler than a man, 153

Kingdom Hall, 82–4

Leaves of brown they fall to the ground, 264
Let us free you from the pain, 253
Let's go walkin' up that mountainside, 305
Lifetimes, 289–90
The light is fading in the afternoon, 353
Like a full force gale, 297
Like to tell you 'bout my baby, 16
Linden Arden Stole the Highlights, 271
Linden Arden stole the highlights, 271
Listen to the Lion, 60–1
Little Village, 398–9
Little village baby, ain't large enough to be a town, 398
Look at the ivy on the old clinging wall, 66
Look Beyond the Hill, 429
Lord have mercy! Feel so good, 372
Lord, if I ever needed someone I need you, 255
Lost in a strange city, nowhere to turn, 203
Love Is Hard Work, 441–2
Love is hard work that's a fact, 441

Madame George, 35–7
Madame Joy, 183–5
Magic Time, 407–8
Man can be king, 419
Man Has to Struggle, 388–9
Man makes his money and they call him rich, 388
Meaning of Loneliness, 203–4
Mechanical Bliss, 267–8
Mechanical bliss is striking me for what I believe in, 267
Meet Me in the Indian Summer, 382–3
Memories, 155–6
Memories, 155
Memory Lane, 430–1
Men saw the stars at the edge of the sea, 293
Moondance, 41–2
My Lonely Sad Eyes, 18
My pagan heart, 424
Mystic Eyes, 19
Mystic of the East, 213
Mystic of the East, mystic from the streets, 213

Naked in the Jungle, 186
Naked in the jungle, naked to the world, 186
Natalia, 287–8
No Religion, 172–3
No use feeling sad, 421
Northern Muse (Solid Ground), 312
Not Supposed to Break Down, 181–2
Now baby just lately you've been holding back too much, 348
Now listen, Julie baby, 23

Oh ain't it lonely when you're living with a gun, 272
Oh fame, they've taken everything and twisted it, 403
Oh my dear, oh my dear sweet love, 164
Oh oh oh ain't gonna moan no more, 439
Oh the mud splattered victims, 355

Oh the smell of the bakery from across the street, 112
Oh the Warm Feeling, 316
Oh the warm feeling, 316
Oh won't you stay, stay awhile, 141
On a golden autumn day, 148
On a golden autumn day returning, 359
On Hyndford Street, 166–7
Once in a Blue Moon, 400
Once in a blue moon, 400
One Irish Rover, 129
One man's meat is another man's poison, 206
One more coffee, one more cigarette, 233
One Sunday mornin', 19
One Two Brown Eyes, 232
Open the Door (to Your Heart), 416–17
Open the door to your heart, 416
Open your arms in the early mornin', 307
Orangefield, 148–9
Out on the highways and the byways all alone, 192

Pagan Heart, 424–6
Pagan Streams, 343
Pay the Devil, 206
The Pen Is Mightier than the Sword, 432–3
Perfect Fit, 350–1
Philosopher's Stone, 192–3
Philosophy, 20
Piper at the Gates of Dawn, 361–2
The photographer smiles, 49
Precious Time, 378–9
Precious time is slipping away, 378
Professional Jealousy, 334–5
Professional jealousy can bring down a nation, 334
The Prophet Speaks, 444
Put on your lipstick, 301

Queen of the Slipstream, 319–20

Rave on, John Donne/Rave on, Part Two, 119–22
Rave on, John Donne, rave on, thy holy fool, 119
Real, Real Gone, 328–9
Real, real gone, 328
Redwood Tree, 262–3
Retreat and View, 422–3
River of Time, 116
Rolling Hills, 89–90
Rough God Goes Riding, 355–6

Saint Dominic's Preview, 62–4
Satisfied, 305–6
Say you wanna be in show business, 189
See Me Through Part II (Just a Closer Walk with Thee), 158–9
Send Your Mind, 28–9
Send your mind, send your mind, 28
A Sense of Wonder, 314–15
She Gives Me Religion, 110
Show Business, 189–91
Showed me pictures in the gallery, 123
Slim Slow Slider, 38
Slim slow slider, 38
The Smile You Smile, 235
The smile you smile is you, 235
Snow in San Anselmo, 65
Snow in San Anselmo, 65
So glad to see you, 82
So Quiet in Here, 151–2
Some Peace of Mind, 238
Some people spend their time, 299
Someone Like You, 135–6
Somerset, 202
Sometimes We Cry, 180
Sometimes we know, sometimes we don't, 180
Song of Home, 210–11
Songwriter, 174
Soul, 212
Soul is a feeling, feeling deep within, 212
Spanish Rose, 25–6

Spirit Will Provide, 443
Spirit will provide beyond the lie, 443
Steppin' Out Queen, 301–2
The Story of Them, 13–15
Stranded, 205
Street Choir, 51
Street choir, sing me the song for the new day, 51–2
The Street Only Knew Your Name, 187–8
Streets of Arklow, 273–4
Summertime in England, 97–103
Sweet Thing, 239–40

Take It Where You Find It, 293–6
Take Me Back, 160–2
Take me back, take me way, way, way back, on Hyndford Street, 166
T.B. Sheets, 23–4
Tell me the story now, 129
There are strange things happening every day, 321
There were people on the sidewalks, 363
There's a small cafe on the outskirts of town, 350
There's something going on, 78
These Are the Days, 150
These are the days of the endless summer, 150
These Dreams of You, 248–9
This Has Got to Stop, 207–8
This is a song about your wavelength, 85
This Weight, 357–8
This weight is weighing on my heart, 357
Tir Na Nog, 132–3
Told you, darling, all along, 20
Too Long in Exile, 168–9
Too long in exile, 168
Too Many Myths, 394–5
Too many myths, 394
Tore Down à la Rimbaud, 123–4
A Town Called Paradise, 317–8
Transformation, 434
Troubadours, 303–4
Try for Sleep, 370–1
Tupelo Honey, 53–4
Twenty third of December, covered in snow, 259

Village Idiot, 339–40
Virgo Clowns, 253–4

Waiting Game, 359–60
Warm Love, 66–7
Wasted Years, 170–1
Wasted years being brainwashed by lies, 170
Wavelength, 85–6
The Way Young Lovers Do, 39–40
We didn't know no better and they said it could be worse, 172
We met deep down in Somerset, 202
We shall walk again, all along the lane, 250
We strolled through fields all wet with rain, 39
We were born before the wind, 43
We were standing in the kingdom, 132
We were the war children, 70
Well don't you know, 382
Well I heard the bells ringing, I was thinking about winning, 380
Well, I'm higher, 114
Well, I'm taking some time with my quiet friend, 137
Well I'm thinking about my people and the love that we once had, 437
Well, it's a marvellous night for a moondance, 41
Well, it's written in the wind, 210
Well let them take you for a clown, 277
Well my baby's gone, so's summer, 344
Well, they told me to come on over, 346

Well you've been on a fast train and it's going off the rails, 390
Went out last night walkin', 232
We've got to put our heads together, 285
What Makes the Irish Heart Beat, 198–9
What will it take for them to leave me alone, 396
Whatever Happened to PJ Proby?, 384–5
Whatever happened to PJ Proby?, 384
What's Wrong with This Picture?, 200–1
What's wrong with this picture?, 200
When all the dark clouds roll away, 44
When Heart Is Open, 309–10
When I recall just how it felt, 386
When the Leaves Come Falling Down, 376–7
When the prophet speaks, 444
When you were a child, you were a tomboy, 275
When your troubles are a burden let your mind be still, 429
Whenever God Shines His Light, 143–4
Whenever God shines His light on me, 143
Whenever the sunshine comes through, 261
When friends were friends, 13
When it's not always raining, there'll be days like this, 175
When I was a young boy back in Orangefield, 125
When Llewellyn comes around, 104
When that Evening Sun Goes Down, 55
When too many demands have destroyed all my plans, 209
When you thought I was a stranger, 33
Whinin' Boy Moan, 392–3
Who Drove the Red Sports Car?, 27
Who drove the red sports car from the mansion, 27
Who Was That Masked Man?, 272
Why Must I Always Explain?, 157
Wild Children, 70
Wild Honey, 307–8
Wild Night, 57–8
Will you meet me in the country, 97
The wine beneath the bed, 25
Wonderful Remark, 367

You can make out pretty good, 58
You can take all the tea in China, 53
You Don't Pull No Punches but You Don't Push the River, 275–6
You Gotta Make It Through the World, 277–8
You know, 94
You Know What They're Writing About, 94–6
You Just Can't Win, 233–4
You Make Me Feel So Free, 299–300
You see me on the street, well you guess I'm doing fine, 338
You sit in silence, 289
You wired the trains and went back home to St Clair Shores, 196
Your street, rich street or poor, 187
You're not supposed to be human, 181
You're the queen of the slipstream, 319
Youth of 1000 Summers, 332–3
You've got to live by the pen 'cause it's mightier than the sword, 432